In the Gospel of St. Matthew this phrase comes seven times in quick succession.

Our Lord had called these men blind guides, foolish and blind, and He said they were like whited sepulchers full of dead men's bones on the inside while appearing beautiful on the outside. He called them serpents, a generation of vipers, children of hell. He accused them of religiously donating ten percent of all their income and then caring not for "judgment, and mercy, and faith": straining out a gnat and swallowing a camel. He told the people that the Scribes and Pharisees loved the first places at feasts and the front seats in the synagogues. He accused the Scribes and Pharisees of cheating widows out of their possessions, saying long prayers in their houses trying to appear religious, and so deceiving these women.

All in all, the words of Christ which He spoke openly to His enemies on that final Wednesday were so forthright and cutting and forceful that one cannot imagine any that would be more definite. They were deserved, but they fanned the flame of their injured pride and anger to a white heat. When the Sanhedrin met that night, the members determined to have their plans of having Jesus put to death carried out at the first opportunity. However, since they feared a possible uprising of His friends, they decided to apprehend Him secretly. It was just about this time that Judas put in his appearance and made his offer.

D1598836

Annas Disconcerted

The next day, Thursday, the plans went into effect. Jesus was taken a prisoner late in the evening in the Garden of Olives. He was hustled off to appear before Annas, the former high priest. In the meantime, the members of the Sanhedrin could be alerted and assembled.

The cunning old Annas asked questions, trying to find out what this young wonder-worker and teacher taught. But all Jesus answered was: "I have spoken openly to the world: I have always taught in the synagogue, and in the temple, whither all the Jews resort, and in secret I have spoken nothing. Why askest thou me? Ask them who have heard what I spoke unto them." (*John* 18:20-21). Annas, who had hoped for statements to refute, found himself disconcerted, with nothing to say. One of the servants came to his rescue by slapping Jesus across the face, exclaiming: "Answerest thou the high priest so?" (*John* 18:22). Jesus reminded this man calmly that this blow proved nothing. "If I have spoken evil, give testimony of the evil; but if well, why strikest thou me?" (*John* 18:23). By this time the Sanhedrin had assembled, and Jesus was led away to appear before that official body with Caiphas at its head.

Caiphas Triumphs

The plan of the enemies of Christ was not just to have Him put to death, but to disgrace Him in the eyes of the people by public trial and official execution. That is why witnesses and formal judgment were required. Many witnesses were brought in and examined, each separately, according to law. But their testimony did not agree. The judges were disappointed. Finally, two witnesses did agree in alleging that Jesus had said: *I will* destroy this temple and in three days build another. This was false, since He had actually said: "Destroy this temple, and in three days I will raise it up." (*John* 2:19). But to all the charges Jesus remained silent.

Then Caiphas asked: "Answerest thou nothing to the things that are laid to thy charge by these men?" (*Mark* 14:60). When Our Lord still made no answer, Caiphas adjured Him by the living God to say whether or not He was the Son of God. This Jesus answered by saying: "I am. And you shall see the Son of man sitting on the right hand of the power of God, and coming with the clouds of heaven." (*Mark* 14:62). At this declaration Caiphas dramatically tore his high-priestly garments and called on all the members of the Sanhedrin to mark the blasphemy. The assembly agreed: He is guilty of death. This brought the session to a close.

However, since these proceedings had taken place during the night and were therefore illegal, the Sanhedrin met right after daybreak and brought Our Lord again before them. He had spent the night at the tender mercy of the guards, who had insulted Him, spat on Him, struck Him. At daybreak, the decision of the night was for-

mally ratified. Jesus, a condemned prisoner with
His hands bound, was led forth. The highest official body of the Jewish people handed over their
Messias to Pilate, the Roman procurator. Blindness, perversity and injustice had triumphed.

The trial before Pilate is the story of browbeat-
ing and forcing a magistrate into a decision he
does not want to make and does not believe in.
Left to himself, Pilate would never have sen-
tenced Christ. He gave in to threats against his
own position. He cannot therefore be excused, but
the active workers for execution were Caiphas
and the chief priests, Scribes and leaders of the
Jewish people.

An Evil Victory Brings No Joy

But even in the midst of their triumph, the enemies of Christ had to swallow a bitter pill. It was
customary to put over the head of a crucified person the reason for the execution. Pilate had a sign
made which read in Latin, Hebrew and Greek:
"Jesus of Nazareth, King of the Jews." When the
chief priests protested to Pilate that the sign
should read not The King of the Jews, but: "He
said, I am the King of the Jews," Pilate answered
decisively: *Quod scripsi, scripsi*—"What I have
written, I have written." (*John* 19:21-22). The
Jewish leaders had had their way in obtaining the
death penalty, but ironically, the inscription over
the Prisoner's head would publicly affirm the very
thing that His enemies had wanted to deny.

One more request was made of Pilate: to give a guard (i.e., a band of guards) to watch over the tomb of Christ. The enemies of Jesus were going to make very sure that no trick would be pulled to make it appear that He had risen; they knew that He had promised to rise. But in providing for the tomb to be guarded, Our Lord's enemies actually worked against themselves, for they thereby put unimpeachable witnesses of the Resurrection at the site of the sepulcher. In fact, later, on Sunday, they had to bribe the soldiers to lie, to say that the Apostles had stolen the body of Christ. "Say you, his disciples came by night, and stole him away when we were asleep. And if the governor shall hear of this, we will persuade him, and secure you." (*Matt.* 28:13-14).

A few years after this, Caiphas was deposed from his office of high priest by demand of the people. That is the last we know of him. Forty years later, as foretold by Our Lord, the Romans took Jerusalem after a long, stubborn siege; they were so angry at the resistance that they crucified Jews until they ran out of trees, fastening them in many cases by twos to the same cross. The rest of the people were put to the sword. The city was leveled. Jesus wept over the coming destruction of Jerusalem. (*Luke* 19:41-42). Those who follow Him will also weep over Jerusalem and over the sufferings of nations and individuals brought on by the disorder of sin. We may well recall here the Peace Plan of Our Lady of Fatima and the tears shed by her statues.

Sometimes we may wonder at the success of the wicked in our own world today. False philosophies hold forth; men of violence and low morals get ahead; nations that defy God advance in their evil designs. God often does not prevent evils, even as He did not stop the enemies of Christ from fulfilling their plans.

But there will always be a day of reckoning for everyone and for every nation. Sometimes there is punishment even in this world. But in the end, the justice of God is satisfied. *We must never be overawed at the sight of the temporary, worldly success of the wicked.* For one day, all the good will receive their just reward, and all the evil will receive their just punishment.

∾ 4 ∾

ST. JOHN THE APOSTLE

AT the traditional Latin Mass, the Scriptural passage read at the very end is the beginning of the Gospel according to St. John. To anyone who is familiar with these words, their sublimity is evident. The style is elevated, balanced and musical. Even a child remembers and senses the strange depth of such a sentence as: "The Word was made Flesh, and dwelt among us." (*John* 1:14). Like all of Scripture, this Gospel is inspired by God, but the thoughts and the style are those of the human writer. The writer of the fourth Gospel is pictured in art as an eagle, because of the heights to which he soars.

St. Augustine says: "What height can bear comparison with that to which this genius ascends? John soars beyond the summits of earth, ethereal space, starry regions, even the celestial choirs and the angelical legions."

St. John's Gospel was the last one written. It was written at the request of Christians who wanted John to refute the Gnostics of the time, who did not believe in the divinity of Christ. It seems no exaggeration to say that not only did St. John incomparably proclaim the divinity of Christ, but he also showed in this Gospel the

heart of Christ more so than does any other piece
of Scriptural writing.

The Beloved Disciple

St. John does not refer to himself by name in
the Gospel, but calls himself either "that other
disciple" or "the disciple whom Jesus loved." He
did have a special place in the affections of Christ.
When he wrote the Gospel many years after
Christ had left this earthly scene, that thought
was still fresh in his mind. St. John is often
referred to as "the beloved disciple." In the popu-
lar mind, the picture of St. John that stands out is
that of him leaning against the breast of Our Lord
at the Last Supper.

Along with Peter and James, John made up the
chosen three among the twelve Apostles. These
three were the elect among the elect. They were
the only ones permitted to go with Our Lord
when He raised the daughter of Jairus to life.
They were the three present at the Transfigura-
tion on Mount Thabor. They were the three whom
Christ took with Him to be near the place where
He prayed in the Garden of Gethsemani. On that
night we find Him alone in prayer, then next to
Him the three, and somewhat farther away the
other Apostles. Here is a demonstration of how
love and loyalty should be divided. There is something touching and comforting in the example of
Our Lord, who while He loved all His Apostles,
yet without injustice to any of the others, gave

privileges to whom He would and selected some for a deeper friendship.

St. John and St. Andrew, before coming to follow Christ, had previously been disciples of John the Baptist. Of the Apostles, these two were the first to meet Jesus after He had begun His public life. Neither lost any time in sharing the good news. It is a sign of their simplicity and family loyalty that they hurried off to find their brothers. Andrew brought his brother, Simon Peter; John went to get his brother, James, to bring him to the One whom John the Baptist had pointed out as the Lamb of God.

John was probably a second cousin of Jesus through his mother, Salome, she and the Blessed Virgin being related. John's father, Zebedee, was a fisherman of some importance. Perhaps James and John had known Jesus before He began His public life. However, they lived at Bethsaida, which was a good day's journey from Nazareth. In those days, visiting at such a distance was not common. (By automobile today, an equivalent trip would mean an eight-hour drive.) The families may have met on the way to Jerusalem for the prescribed pilgrimages.

Sons of Thunder

St. John is usually pictured as a young man. He was most likely younger than both Jesus and his own brother, James. Because of his reputation as the beloved disciple, some people think of John as effeminate. He was certainly not that. In fact, he and James earned a nickname from Our Lord: "the Sons of Thunder." Whether this title was given because of their fiery temperament or their manner of speaking is not known. But it indicates characters of proper manly strength.

John interrupted a discourse of Christ one day to tell Him that a man had been casting out devils in His name and that he and the others had forbidden him. Our Lord answered: "Do not forbid him. For there is no man that doth a miracle in my name, and can soon speak ill of me." (*Mark* 9:38). John's interruption here indicates an eager, ardent temperament. On another occasion, James and John wanted to call down fire from Heaven to destroy a Samaritan town that had not welcomed Christ. They were both rebuked for this. "You know not of what spirit you are. The Son of man came not to destroy souls, but to save." (*Luke* 9:55-56).

A Mother's Request

Salome, the mother of James and John, was one of the devoted women who often followed Jesus and the Apostles to provide for their material needs. As Jesus was going up to Jerusalem and after He had just predicted His sufferings, death and Resurrection, Salome approached Him and made a request: "Say that these my two sons may sit, the one on thy right hand, and the other on thy left, in thy kingdom." (*Matt.* 20:21). The two sons must have had some idea of what their mother was asking. They were close at hand. When Christ asked: "Can you drink the chalice that I shall drink," they gave a very simple and direct answer. "We can," they said. (*Matt.* 20:22). Our Lord told them they did not know what they were asking for. They would indeed drink of the cup of suffering. However, to sit at His right hand or left hand belonged to those for whom it was prepared by the Father.

The forwardness of the two brothers in this incident earned them the indignation of the other ten Apostles. Jesus finally gathered them all around Himself and told them: "You know that the princes of the Gentiles lord it over them; and they that are the greater, exercise power upon them. It shall not be so among you: but whosoever will be the greater among you, let him be your minister: and he that will be first among you, shall be your servant." (*Matt.* 20:25-27). They should be like the Son of Man, who came not to be served but to serve and to give His life as a ransom for many.

Holy Thursday

On the day of the Last Supper, it was Peter and John who were sent into the city to prepare the place of the Paschal meal. At the meal itself, John was next to Our Lord. When Jesus predicted that one of them would betray Him, Peter asked John to find out who it was. John, leaning confidently back on the bosom of Jesus, asked: "Lord, who is it?" (*John* 13:25). Evidently the answer, that it was the one who would be handed the morsel of bread dipped, was heard only by John, because the other Apostles did not know why Judas left shortly afterward.

During the Agony in the Garden, Peter, James and John were told to watch and pray along with their Master. But in the weakness of the flesh, they kept falling asleep. We can not help making the comparison between the sublime John of the Gospel and *Apocalypse* and the sleepy John of the Garden.

After the arrest of Jesus, John went into the palace of Caiphas to watch the proceedings. He had free access and was not harrassed, although Peter was. Some have surmised that John's connection with this place began when in earlier days he had delivered fish to the high priest's house.

"Behold Thy Son."

On Good Friday afternoon, we see John, the Beloved Disciple, alone of all the Apostles standing at the foot of the Cross. Salome, his mother, was also there. During the three long hours of darkness and bitter suffering, Jesus spoke but few words. Yet as He hung there on the Cross, He thought of the future of His Mother here on the earth. St. Joseph had evidently already died, and there were no other children to take care of the Blessed Virgin Mary. So in the midst of redeeming all the people of the earth, Our Lord took the time, as a dutiful Son, to provide for the welfare of His Mother. He looked at her and said: "Woman, behold thy son." Then He said to John: "Behold thy mother." (*John* 19:26-27).

Our Lord left the guidance of the Church to Peter; to John He left the care and protection of His Mother. Throughout the rest of her earthly days, St. John provided for Mary as a son would for his mother. What a privilege it would have been to listen to the conversation of these two in the ensuing years as they recalled the words and deeds of Jesus!

After Peter

On the morning of the Resurrection, after Mary Magdalen had reported that the body of the Lord was not at the tomb, both Peter and John ran together to the tomb, but John outdistanced Peter and arrived first. He says very plainly in the Gospel, "that other disciple did outrun Peter, and came first to the sepulchre." (*John* 20:4). It almost sounds as if John were making a point of a personal triumph, he is so definite. But when he arrived there, in deference to the Head of the Apostles, John did not enter the sepulcher, but waited, and Peter went in first. Then John followed.

The Only Apostle Not Martyred

Among the early Christians, there grew up a saying that John would never die. This was based on a prophecy of Our Lord which they misinterpreted. Jesus had told Peter that he would be executed. Then Peter, seeing John walking behind them asked: "Lord, and what shall this man do?" (*John* 21:21). The answer was: "So I will have him to remain till I come, what is it to thee?" (*John* 21:22). John in his Gospel states that Christ did not predict that he would never die. "Jesus did not say to him: He should not die; but, So I will have him to remain till I come, what is it to thee?" (*John* 21:23). As far as we know, John was the only one of the Apostles who died a natural death. His brother James, for instance, was put to death early, being beheaded under Herod Agrippa on April 1, A.D. 42, according to the Roman Breviary.

Although John worked in establishing the Church first in Palestine, he spent the greatest part of his life overseeing the churches which had been established in Asia Minor. His ordinary abode was probably Hierapolis in Phrygia, which was in the center of his jurisdiction. Later, he came to live at Ephesus with the Blessed Mother.

He had powerful enemies in the magicians, e.g., Appolonius of Tyana. Perhaps, in his courageous opposition to these men, he demonstrated only too well his right to the title of Son of Thunder. In time, the opposition became strong enough that he was sent to Rome to appear before the Emperor Domitian. In cruelty, Domitian was superior to the better known Nero. According to Tertullian, Domitian ordered John to be plunged into a cauldron of boiling oil, but St. John stepped out of the boiling oil unharmed. So Domitian had him banished to the island of Patmos. There St. John wrote that mysterious book known as the *Apocalypse,* the last book of the Bible. It contains passages of beauty, full of the essence of truth, comforting to the soul. At the same time it is a book of visions and prophecy, often very difficult to understand or interpret. On the death of Domitian, St. John returned to Ephesus.

Old Age

Two stories of John's final years have come down to us from the Fathers of the Church. St. Clement of Alexandria relates that St. John's attention was once drawn to a certain young man in the congregation. He presented the young man to the Bishop of that place. The Bishop instructed him, then baptized and confirmed him. Later, the young man fell into bad company and became a robber. When St. John returned later and learned of this, he went out on horseback to the mountain where the robbers lived, where he was taken prisoner. He told the captors that he had come purposely to be made a prisoner in order that he might be led to the young man. When the young man saw St. John, he tried to slip away in shame. But John called out for him not to run away from his father, but to repent. The young man threw away his arms, burst into tears, and St. John reconciled him to God. Thus, even as an old man, this Apostle could still be so concerned over one soul as to risk his life to save it.

St. Jerome has written that when John was old and no longer able to preach, he would be carried to the assembly of the Faithful, where every time he said the same words: "My little children, love one another." When his hearers grew somewhat weary and finally asked why he said the same thing each time, he replied: "Because it is the word of the Lord, and if you keep it, you do enough."

St. John died around the year A.D. 100, probably about the age of 94. He died at Ephesus and was buried there.

The first church erected over his tomb was destroyed by an earthquake. The second was changed into a mosque. A humble chapel has replaced the second splendid basilica. Many pilgrims visit St. John's tomb there.

St. John Shows the Heart of Christ

Men have always tried to remake Jesus Christ according to their own hearts. Sentimentalists make Him a sentimentalist. Rigorists want to make Him too stern. Today, especially, many want a kind of hollow Christ, a symbol of what is good and noble and right, according to their conception of the ideal man. But the depth of truth that Christ taught, its drastic call to action and His very divinity—these they want left out.

St. John leaned on the Heart of Christ at the Last Supper. He showed the Heart of Christ in his Gospel and in the first of his three Epistles. More so than any other writer, St. John showed Our Lord as entirely and beautifully human. Yet more than any other, he also showed Our Lord to be divine, the true Son of God. He presents the complete Christ. We should read and reread St. John's Gospel, Epistles and *Apocalypse* in order truly to understand Christ.

SIMON OF CYRENE

THE name of Simon of Cyrene and his bearing of the Cross for Christ is mentioned by three of the Gospel writers, Matthew, Mark and Luke. There is something dramatic about this man who suddenly walked, in one moment, from unknown into undying remembrance. Nobody had ever heard of him before, and most likely nobody ever *would* have heard of Simon of Cyrene. But one day he happened along at just the right time, and today, more than nineteen centuries later, we all know his name. It is inscribed in our churches under the Fifth Station, and every time we make the Way of the Cross we repeat his name.

How many great scholars are forgotten! How many generals and statesmen who wielded immense power, who marched in grand triumph are unremembered! How many ambitious men of all ages have tried mightily for an immortal name on the earth and scarcely became known to their own generations! Today, there are many who would like to go down in history, but despite their present reputation or notoriety, in fifty years they will at best be buried in the footnotes of dusty volumes, their names scarcely glanced at by research scholars. On Good Friday afternoon, a man who had no earthly power, who was not ambitious or scholarly, was unwillingly pushed into the living pages of history.

Christ Was Exhausted

Ordinarily it was less difficult for the condemned man to carry his cross to the place of execution. He carried the cross or the crosspiece, the *patibulum,* and only after arrival at the spot outside the city was he scourged. But Christ had already been scourged, whipped by the sharp lashes that bit into His flesh. Besides, He had been crowned with thorns. He had been made sport of, spat upon, struck on His crowned head and on His face with a stick. The night before, He had undergone extreme mental agony. That alone was exhausting, for heavy sorrow tires the body. He had not had any sleep during the whole night, but had spent that time standing before the unjust judges. When He started out for Calvary, He was already completely exhausted. His strength was drained. Twenty-four hours before, the burden of the *patibulum* would have been bearable. Now it was an enormous task just to walk to the hill called Calvary. Our Lord was like a man who has had an operation or whose system has experienced some profound physical shock. Even to walk a short distance leaves such a person worn and gasping for breath.

Because of His weakened condition, Our Lord

fell to the ground. How many times He fell altogether is not known. The Stations of the Cross picture just three falls. Various traditions count between three and seven falls.

Did Simon Show Pity?

Perhaps we may reconstruct the scene. The soldiers wanted to get their job done—not that they had anything else important to do, but like any rough, healthy men, they soon lost patience with a stumbling, falling man. Simon of Cyrene just then came along, returning from the country. Perhaps he indicated some pity for the crushed, beaten carrier of the Cross. Perhaps he made some remark that was overheard by the soldiers. Perhaps there was some reason why they singled him out and forced him to help. There were dozens of others who could have served just as well.

Earlier, the crown of thorns had been thought up by the soldiers as a jest. Now they added another bit of improvised merriment. It would be a joke to make this sympathetic Simon play the role of a condemned criminal. Besides, they would get to their destination sooner and get the job done. Why should they wait for this weary King of the Jews to get back His breath and His strength? On to the top of the hill and a refreshing drink of wine!

Artists have pictured Simon as carrying part of the Cross, as though he carried one end and Christ carried the other. The words of the Gospel are not entirely clear: "And going out, they found a man of Cyrene, named Simon: him they forced to take up his cross." (*Matt.* 27:32). "They laid the cross on him to carry after Jesus." (*Luke* 23:26). The word used for cross is *patibulum,* which really means the crosspiece. Whatever it was—the Cross as pictured in traditional art, or the crossbeam—Simon himself bore at least part of the burden.

Cyrene was a Greek city in what is now Libya in northern Africa. Either Simon had personally lived there, or his ancestors had. In any case, people knew him as Simon the Cyrenean, although he may have been a Jew. Most likely, he now lived in Jerusalem, since at the time he was returning from the fields. He had probably been working there.

St. Mark mentions the names of the two sons of Simon: Rufus and Alexander. (*Mark* 15:21). In the course of time, these two became Christians, along with their mother and Simon himself. They are spoken of several times later in the New Testament. It is interesting to note that the mother was so beloved by St. Paul that he refers to her as his own mother: "Salute Rufus, elect in the Lord, and his mother and mine." (*Rom.* 16:13).

Simon Was Unwilling

Simon of Cyrene may have been a kind-hearted man. He may have had pity for the man he was being forced to help. Still, Simon was forced. He did not take up the Cross willingly.

Not even St. John had thought of doing that or
had offered to do so. To carry the cross was an
unspeakable disgrace. The cross was for the low-
est criminals, slaves and murderers. The one who
carried it was the one who died on it in disgrace.
Simon had to carry the hated object and still live
on. Perhaps in his mind there burned the
thought of his present shame, and perhaps he
looked ahead to future years when people might
point and say: "He's the one who carried a cross,"
either in open mockery or in whispered secrecy.

Whether Simon marched the whole way in bitter inner protest or received the grace of joy and
understanding as he went along is a matter of
surmise. He and his family were fully rewarded in
due time by the gift of the Christian faith.

No Mere Accident

This extraordinary event of Simon and the
Cross must have an important meaning for all of
us. Nothing connected with the Passion and
Death of Christ was purely accidental. Many of
the seemingly minor details were fulfillments of
ancient prophecies. What is the meaning of
Simon's helping to carry the Cross of Christ?

The answer may be seen in what Our Lord said
while instructing the Apostles before sending
them forth to preach, to cure, and to cast out devils. "He that loveth father or mother more than
me, is not worthy of me, and he that loveth son or
daughter more than me, is not worthy of me. And

he that taketh not up his cross, and followeth me, is not worthy of me. He that findeth his life, shall lose it: and he that shall lose his life for me, shall find it." (*Matt.* 10:37-39). Again, the answer may be seen in what St. Paul said: "[I] now rejoice in my sufferings for you, and fill up those things that are wanting of the sufferings of Christ, in my flesh, for his body, which is the church." (*Col.* 1:24).

Simon of Cyrene walking after Christ is the living symbol of the way all must walk who want to follow Our Lord. "He that taketh not up his cross, and followeth me, is not worthy of me." (*Matt.* 10:38). Simon helping Christ is again the living symbol of all who help accomplish the Redemption by willing suffering.

We All Must Help to Carry the Cross

In short, Simon's helping Our Lord shows that in God's unfathomable plans for saving souls, we must all bear our crosses. Our own salvation and that of others depend on our participation in the Passion and Death of Jesus Christ. We have to help Jesus bear His Cross.

Certainly, on the first Good Friday, Christ, being God, could have, in His divine power, walked easily, carrying His Cross and not falling. But, He did not. He allowed his humanity to bear the burden and Simon to help. Certainly too, His sacrifice on Calvary in itself is infinite and requires no help from any of us. But

God does not apply this saving sacrifice unless there are others who "help" Him by also carrying at least part of the Cross. In God's plan, *we have to help.*

This is a profound truth. Anybody who comes to understand it well has solved the riddle of all the disappointments, setbacks, sorrows and sufferings of life.

All of us are like Simon because we have to help. Most of us are like him in another way, too because we receive the cross unwillingly. It may be forced upon us, even as on Simon, by those who are crucifying Christ. We may be the victims of the sins of others, of defamation of character by speech, of less-than-human hatred, of obstinacy and cruelty. We may be crushed by the misunderstanding of those who should love us. Or our cross may be pain of body. It may be the even worse pain of "nerves" and emotional suffering. Whatever the cross is, it usually finds us at first unwilling. But whatever it is, it can lead us to final fulfillment and salvation, as it did for Simon of Cyrene and his family.

Spiritual Success

Lydia Longley has a right to the title, "the First American nun." She was the first girl born in the limits of the present United States to enter a convent. But if it had not been for a very tragic event, she might have died in Groton, Massachusetts, as a Puritan, without even knowing the graces of the

Catholic Faith. In 1684 an Indian raiding party killed her father, her stepmother, and five other members of her family. She was taken into captivity into what is now Montreal. There she was ransomed by a French family. She found friendship, and much more, the Catholic Faith. Later she entered the convent of the Congregation of Notre Dame.

Lydia Longley had been carried away by Indians at the age of twenty. At twenty-two she embraced the Faith. At twenty-five she took her final vows as a nun. She lived the religious life for many years, and finally went to her reward in 1758. She is buried in Montreal. The heavy cross that she had to carry brought the gift of faith and of a religious vocation.

St. Pius X came from a family that bore the cross of real poverty. When he was going to high school in Castelfranco, he was up before dawn to serve the early Mass. Then he walked three miles to school. Usually he stopped right outside of town and took off his shoes and slung them about his neck by the shoestrings. This he did to keep them from wearing out. At the noon hour he tutored some children, in return for which the mother of the family gave him his lunch. In the late afternoon, he walked the three miles back home to Riese. This was what the future Pope and Saint had to do in order to continue his education toward his goal of the priesthood. But the cross of poverty helped him to develop a kind and sympathetic heart for others. It helped him to develop self-forgetfulness and the spirit of sacrifice, which led him to sainthood.

In his case, in that of Lydia Longley, and in countless others, we can see how God laid a cross on the Saints. We can also see how it led to growth in holiness and to salvation.

Sickness unto the Glory of God

Our Lord spoke very plainly about the sickness of Lazarus. His words are striking: "This sickness is not unto death, but for the glory of God: that the Son of God may be glorified by it." (*John* 11:4). Lazarus endured the pains of his illness. He actually went through the final pain of death. His sisters Martha and Mary, so dear to Our Lord, suffered the heavy sorrow of the loss of their brother. When Our Lord finally came, both Martha and Mary told Him confidently that if only He had been there, their brother would not have died. Yet Our Lord's absence had been deliberate. Though He later wept at the tomb of Lazarus, He actually rejoiced when He told the Apostles that Lazarus had died. He said: "I am glad, for your sakes, that I was not there, that you may believe." (*John* 11:15). Lazarus suffered and died; his sisters sorrowed; yet Christ, who loved the three of them so much, rejoiced because of the good that His raising of Lazarus would do for the faith of the Apostles.

The illness of Lazarus took place so that the Son of Man might be glorified. All the trials and sicknesses of life can serve the same purpose. Often we cannot see in our own lives how this works out. In some cases the results will be known only in Heaven. But whenever we have a cross to bear we should remember Simon of Cyrene. He too was unwilling, but he obtained the grace of conversion. If we carry our crosses as Simon did, recognizing them as the cross of Christ, walking after Him, then every cross will help us on to our salvation. It will also help us help others to reach Heaven.

The Cross of Christ meant the salvation of all men. Simon helped carry that Cross. We are like Simon when we take up our cross as the Cross of Christ. It seemed that Simon came accidentally on the scene. Our crosses seem so accidental and unnecessary. Yet that accidental cross is no accident at all, but a wonderful favor from God. It can mean that our names are written in the Book of Life.

ST. MARY MAGDALEN

AFTER He began His public life, Our Lord had no fixed residence. When a Scribe one day wanted to follow Him, He warned the man: "The foxes have holes, and the birds of the air nests: but the son of man hath not where to lay his head." (*Matt.* 8:20). Many times Our Lord spent the night out in the open. There were places, however, in which He accepted hospitality. His favorite stopping place was the home of Martha and Mary, two sisters, and their brother, Lazarus, in Bethany.

There is never mention of a mother in this family. She was most likely deceased. The father likewise was either deceased or is to be identified with Simon the Leper, who may have been living, but was separated from ordinary society because of his disease. At any rate, Martha was the mistress of the house. It was to this house at Bethany, less than two miles (fifteen stadia) from Jerusalem, that the Saviour came on many occasions to relax from the labors of His preaching and traveling, or to find shelter when in danger from enemies. He and His Apostles were always made welcome and given food and lodging. The two sisters were devoted to Christ, and it was a happy occasion for everyone when He came to partake of their hospitality.

A Pound of Nard

It was at this home that Our Lord spent the last six days of His life before the Passion. He went into Jerusalem on Palm Sunday, and again several times during the week, returning to spend the night at Bethany. On Saturday, the day after His arrival and the day before Palm Sunday, a banquet was prepared in His honor in the house of Simon the Leper. This could be the home of Martha and Mary, if Simon was their father.

During the course of the evening Mary decided to do something extraordinary to manifest her reverence and love for Christ. She came in with an alabaster vase of the most exquisite perfume. It was costly nard (spikenard). In those days it was customary for the host to honor his guests by pouring on their heads a sweet-scented oil. What Mary was about to do was not in its essence unusual. However, to use a whole pound of the most precious kind of perfume *was* unusual. This represented the value of an ordinary workman's earnings for almost a year. Translated into our day, it would be all that a laborer, a store clerk or a taxi driver could buy with his year's wages. Mary broke the long, slender neck of the bottle and poured out the costly oil over the head of Christ. Then, in a gesture of great humility, she poured the remainder over His feet, loosened the long tresses of her hair, and with them wiped His blessed feet.

The delightful odor of the nard filled the whole house. But while great souls like Mary's never think of the cost when they want to show their love, more narrow souls have to measure everything in terms of money. So a complaint went up, voiced by a number of the people present. Judas Iscariot asked openly: "Why was not this ointment sold for three hundred pence, and given to the poor?" (*John* 12:5). Christ defended the action of Mary saying: "Why do you trouble this woman? for she hath wrought a good work upon me. For the poor you have always with you: but me you have not always. For she, in pouring this ointment upon my body, hath done it for my burial. Amen I say to you, wheresoever this gospel shall be preached in the whole world, that also which she hath done, shall be told for a memory of her." (*Matt.* 26:10-13).

One Woman or Three?

Who was this woman who was so devoted to Christ and so extravagant in showing her love and respect? We would like to give a simple, unchallengeable answer and say that Mary of Bethany is none other than Mary Magdalen. But the point has been argued back and forth since the fourth century. Besides the anointing by Mary, the sister of Martha, the Gospel speaks of another anointing by an unnamed, sinful woman, who had poured oil over His feet at an earlier date. In the Eastern or

Greek rites of the Church, three women are distinguished: Mary of Bethany, Mary Magdalen and the unnamed sinner. Three separate feasts are celebrated for these three. Following the weighty scholarship of St. Gregory the Great, the Western or Latin rite of the Church has traditionally identified both Mary of Bethany and the nameless, sinful woman with Mary Magdalen. In the *Roman Breviary,* the prayer for the Feast day of Mary Magdalen, July 22, identifies her with Mary, the sister of Lazarus. The antiphon for First Vespers completes the circle by identifying her with the unnamed, sinful woman.

Whatever the case may be, combining all the incidents and referring them to Mary Magdalen does no violence to, but rather better illustrates her character and disposition. All that is said of Mary of Bethany and the unnamed sinner harmonizes with the unique relationship that existed between Our Lord and Mary Magdalen.

Mary Magdalen's early history is not known definitely, but according to the tradition of the Jewish rabbis, she had been married to one of the officers of Herod's court. With him she had gone to live at Magdala, a city on the western shore of the Lake of Genesareth. She was a woman of great physical beauty, and she also possessed of rare gifts of intelligence and social ability. Whether her husband was jealous or was himself unfaithful, or whatever the cause, Mary had gone from coquetry to dalliance to sin. Once she had fallen, she plunged on and on. She obtained a divorce, spurned public opinion, and lived the life of a high-class prostitute. She was of good station and a wealthy family. Her object was not money, but pleasure and the intoxication of making men pay tribute to her. This life she led at the city of Magdala, from which her name of Magdalen is taken. No details are mentioned in the Gospel concerning a marriage or even a sinful life. The Gospel says simply that seven devils had gone out of Mary Magdalen. (*Luke* 8:2).

Kisses and Tears

The city of Magdala at the foot of a steep mountain and next to the lake shore was surrounded by the beauties of nature, but according to the ancient rabbis, it was wicked. It was here that Mary Magdalen would have been delivered of the seven devils by Jesus. (*Mark* 16:9). Not long after this, He was invited to a supper by a Pharisee named Simon. Mary Magdalen came into the banquet hall, drawing the eyes of all to herself. She was known to all as a public sinner; the people present did not know that she had already come under the influence of Our Lord and had decided to lead a different life.

On this occasion Mary braved the sneering remarks and the haughty glances to come to the feet of Christ. She wept copious tears, which fell upon His feet, and she wiped them with her long hair. She kissed His feet and anointed them with ointment. In ancient times in Palestine, women always went about with their heads covered. If a woman was guilty of unchastity and came to the Jewish priest to repent, he unloosed her hair, which was a sign of humiliation, and gave her a bitter potion to drink.

Mary Magdalen's actions, then, were purposely humiliating to herself. She had been a public sinner, so she would do public penance. She had disregarded public opinion in her life of sin, so she disregarded public opinion in demonstrating her repentance and her love for Christ. On this occasion she wept. On this occasion she anointed only His feet. The week before the death of Christ she did not weep, and she anointed first His head.

As Mary Magdalen was weeping over the feet of Christ, Simon the Pharisee, the master of the house, thought within himself: "This man, if he were a prophet, would know surely who and what manner of woman this is that toucheth him, that she is a sinner." (*Luke* 7:39). The Pharisees taught that the touch of a public sinner was as foul as that of a leper. Jesus answered the unspoken criticism of the Pharisee by telling him a parable.

"A certain creditor had two debtors, the one owned five hundred pence, and the other fifty. And whereas they had not wherewith to pay, he forgave them both. Which therefore of the two loveth him most?" (*Luke* 7:41-42). Simon answered that he supposed the one to whom more was forgiven. Christ then criticized Simon for neglecting to anoint Him, to provide water for His feet and to give the kiss of welcome. These were customary for an honored guest, but Simon had neglected all of them. Our Lord continued: "but she with tears hath washed my feet, . . . she, since she came in, hath not ceased to kiss my feet . . . she with ointment hath anointed my feet." Therefore "Many sins are forgiven her, because she hath loved much." He then reassured Mary: "Thy sins are forgiven thee." (*Luke* 7:44-48).

And the Last Shall Be First

After this, Mary Magdalen, by the force of her love, her devotedness and her natural intelligence, rose to become, in the eyes of the Apostles, the foremost of that group of holy women who ministered to them and their Master. In the Gospels, her name is given first place among the women. Her place may be compared to that of St. Peter among the men. We except, of course, the Blessed Mother, who is in a unique position of her own and not to be listed with others. Depending on the circumstances, Mary Magdalen and other devoted women went from place to place to do what they could to provide for the comfort of Christ and His Apostles. After her conversion, Mary left Magdala to live with her sister at Bethany.

At the Feet of Christ

It was here one day that the two sisters, Martha and Mary, received Christ and His disciples. They welcomed Him and set about preparing a meal. But when Jesus sat down to instruct the disciples, Mary stopped her part of the work and sat down at His feet to listen. Here is where we always find her, at the feet of Christ. Mary's soul thirsted for the words of wisdom that would make her more worthy of Christ. She did not want to miss anything that He said when He spoke words of instruction and advice.

Martha continued to go about the details of the meal. Then after a while she began to fret over the easy role of her sister, sitting down, listening to the conversation. Martha brought her problem to the chief Guest with a directness that shows how much at home He was in that house: "Lord, hast thou no care that my sister hath left me alone to serve? speak to her therefore, that she help me." (*Luke* 10:40). Instead of receiving any satisfaction, the poor woman received a rebuke: "Martha, Martha, thou art careful, and art troubled about many things: but one thing is necessary. Mary hath chosen the best part, which shall not be taken away from her." (*Luke* 10:41-42).

This is a text that quite a few housewives might well put up in their kitchens. Nourishment for the mind and the soul is more essential than so many details that are worried over and fretted over in the usages of society. Mary had been working, too, to prepare the meal. It was only a few niceties that Martha now hurried over. It was foolish to be concerned over such things and to miss the discourse, which was the best feature of the whole banquet.

On Good Friday, we find Mary Magdalen again at the feet of Jesus. This time those feet were nailed to the Cross, pierced, blood dripping from them slowly to the ground. Mary Magdalen poured no ointment now; but again her tears fell, as they had the first time she had come into the banquet hall. Then they mingled with the ointment; now they mingled with the Precious Blood on the ground beneath the Cross. After the death of Christ, after Joseph of Arimathea had obtained Pilate's permission and had buried the body of the Saviour, Mary Magdalen still remained. She watched the men roll up the large stone, and with Mary, the mother of Joseph, she waited, bowed in grief. (*Mark* 15:47). These two were the last to leave the tomb on Friday evening.

Christ Appears to Her Alone

On Sunday morning, Mary Magdalen was with the first group to arrive at the sepulcher. Saturday was observed according to Jewish law as the Lord's Day. The first to arrive at the sepulcher were the women who were so devoted to Christ. It was Mary Magdalen's quick, lively imagination that took in the empty tomb and made her fear desecration of the body of Jesus by His enemies. She ran back to find Peter and John and told them, "They have taken away the Lord out of the sepulchre, and we know not where they have laid Him." (*John* 20:2).

After Peter and John came and inspected the

empty tomb, Mary Magdalen remained standing outside weeping. After a while, she looked into the tomb and saw two Angels, who asked her: "Woman, why weepest thou?" She answered: "Because they have taken away my Lord; and I know not where they have laid him." (*John* 20:13). Right after this she turned around and saw one whom she took to be the gardener. She was grieving deeply and may not have looked closely. Or, as with others who saw Christ after the Resurrection, the recognition was not always immediate. The one she took for the gardener also asked why she was weeping. She told him: "Sir, if thou hast taken him hence, tell me where thou hast laid him, and I will take him away." (*John* 20:15).

Then Jesus said to her: "Mary." She immediately recognized Him and cried out: "Rabboni!" (which is to say, "Master!"). A woman so fully feminine and so emotionally wrought up had to demonstrate her sudden, overwhelming relief and joy by some sweeping gesture. Once again we find her at the feet of Jesus, where she had leaped and cast herself. No doubt she still wept, but now in the happiness of finding Him alive. He bade her to go and tell His brethren of His coming Ascension into Heaven.

The Greeks hold that Mary Magdalen went to Ephesus with the Blessed Virgin Mary and died there. A French tradition says that she died in France. It is in France, in the district of Provence, that relics claimed to be hers are honored. Many pilgrimages have been made to this place.

The Future Begins Now

No doubt it takes a great soul to be able to understand fully a person like Mary Magdalen. But to everybody, she stands out as the great example of a sinner who became a penitent and a Saint. She made up for her sins by a great love for Our Lord. Never again did she turn back, once she had repented. She plunged into lifelong repentance; she immersed herself entirely in the great love of Jesus Christ. If we have been sinners, we can do the same. If we have been leading moderately good lives, let us remember that someone we now consider a sinner, someone who truly may be a sinner, may end up by being a great Saint, while we continue in mediocrity.

If we want to be great with God, the past does not matter; neither does the present, though we be now steeped in sin. But the future must be filled with a great love for God. And the future must begin right now!

~ 7 ~

THE DEVOTED WOMEN

THE words spoken by Our Lord to the women of Jerusalem are the only recorded words of His from the time He left Pilate's court until He was fixed to the Cross. "Daughters of Jerusalem, weep not over me; but weep for yourselves, and for your children." (*Luke* 23:28). As far as we know, these are the only words Our Lord spoke along the *Via Dolorosa*.

All women can rejoice and take honest pride in the fact that when Our Lord was deserted by His Apostles, representatives of their sex did not fear to show compassion. When Christ was scoffed at, mistreated, condemned and put to death by men, He was not forgotten by those whose natural endowments from their Creator make them more open to pity and sympathy. When many hearts were beating in the excitement of a satisfied hate, some hearts beat with the ache of a sorrow shared. When many eyes burned fiercely as the hardness and vengefulness of bitter souls looked through, some eyes were covered over with tears of compassion.

There were two classes of women who showed affectionate sorrow for Our Lord on Good Friday. There were the women of Galilee who had known

65

Him long and well and had often ministered to His needs, as well as those of the Apostles and disciples. There were also the women of Jerusalem, some of whom may have known Christ fairly well, whereas some perhaps were noticing Him for the first time as a Stranger led forth to death.

A Woman of Courage

It is quite possible that it was a woman from either of these groups who courageously presented a cloth to wipe the face of Christ. "Veronica" could have been the forthright Martha of Bethany, as some have conjectured, or the woman cured of a hemorrhage, or the wife of Zaccheus, as others have proposed, or any woman grateful for some miracle.

The elements of the story of Veronica's Veil as we now have it were not all put together until the fifteenth century. The name "Veronica" means "true image" or "true (*vera*) icon." In the Roman *Ordo* of 1143, the image itself, venerated in Rome, is referred to as *Veronica*. This name could easily have then passed on to become the traditional name of the woman who offered the veil to Our Lord. The Greek name for her is "Berenice," which also means "true image."

Although the Veronica tradition may not meet strict historical criteria, it has endured for hundreds of years and has become sacred through its use in the Stations of the Cross. It illustrates the heart and mind of all the women who showed understanding and sympathy to Our Lord.

Cardinal Gaetano DeLai pictured the story in the following way: The noisy procession wound its way through the narrow streets of Jerusalem. Suddenly, a door opened; a matron with her face veiled, but walking fearlessly, made her way swiftly through the crowd, got past the soldiers, and knelt at the feet of Jesus. Surprised, the crowd stopped; the woman drew forth a linen napkin or towel and offered it to Jesus. He accepted the linen and for an instant pressed it to His bleeding face. It all happened in a moment, while the crowd looked on curiously; the soldiers were momentarily nonplussed. Then the Jewish enemies shout to the soldiers, fearing that a wave of sympathy may rise in favor of Our Lord. The crowd moved on again. Veronica hurried back into her house. She thought to herself how she would preserve this linen all her life. It would be a symbol to her of the precious goodness of the innocent Man who was going out to be crucified. As she reflected, she opened the cloth, and then she saw traced on the cloth the outline of the face of Jesus. Her treasure was of far greater value than she could ever have imagined.

The question naturally arises: What became of this image? Since the haze of history befogs the whole issue, nobody can really say anything with certainty. But in St. Peter's at Rome, in a chapel built into one of the great stone piers that support the dome of the basilica, there is kept the linen which is called the "Sacred Face" and which is traditionally identified with the Cloth of Veronica. It is said that with the passage of so many years, the image is faded.

Tears for Jerusalem

To some of the women of Jerusalem to whom Our Lord spoke, He was fairly well-known; to others a stranger. They, along with a large crowd, were following Him. Probably some of the disciples were in that crowd too. No doubt, in the crowd were some who had heard Him preach, or who had seen or heard of His miracles. They were now following in sorrow. But it was the weeping women who merited to be addressed by the Saviour.

On Palm Sunday, as He came near the city of Jerusalem, it was Christ Himself who had first shed tears. He wept over the city, including for its "daughters" who were now weeping for Him. He grieved because He looked ahead and saw the terrible destruction and punishment that would come upon Jerusalem in 70 A.D. "For the days shall come upon thee, and thy enemies shall cast a trench about thee, and compass thee round, and straiten thee on every side, and beat thee flat to the ground, and thy children who are in thee: and they shall not leave in thee a stone upon a stone: because thou hast not known the time of thy visitation." (*Luke* 19:43-44).

Tears for Christ

Now the women are weeping over Him. Their tears evidence their good hearts and drop as a silent tribute to the goodness of the Sufferer, like the verdict of a people's jury that was never heard on the innocence of Christ. But He over whom the women cry looks from the present into the future. He is thinking of the future destruction of Jerusalem when He tells the women of Jerusalem to weep rather for themselves and for their children. "For behold, the days shall come, wherein they will say: Blessed are the barren, and the wombs that have not borne, and the paps that have not given suck. Then shall they begin to say to the mountains: Fall upon us; and to the hills: Cover us!" (*Luke* 23:29-30).

What Our Lord referred to was the destruction of Jerusalem that would take place in the year A.D. 70 under Vespasian and Titus. As the stubborn siege continued, there was terrible starvation within the city. Gruesome stories have come down, some indicating that even cannibalism was practiced to obtain nourishment. In these days mothers had no food for their children and had to watch them grow thin and sick and die of starvation. Those were the days when mothers would bewail having had children. Ordinarily it was considered a disgrace among Jewish women to be childless, but in such circumstances the prophecy of Christ came true and men said: "Blessed are the barren."

The phrase comes as an ominous echo into our

own times, when immoral avoidance of procreation is so sadly widespread, even among Catholics. "Blessed are the barren" is heard again today.

Jesus ended His address to the daughters of Jerusalem by saying: "For if in the green wood they do these things, what shall be done in the dry?" (*Luke* 23:31). He compares Himself to the green wood. In Scripture an innocent and good man is often compared to a green tree full of life; sinners are compared to dry wood. If such punishment is meted out to Our Lord, what can be expected in the case of sinners?

The Women of Galilee

The other group which showed sorrow for Christ on Good Friday was made up of women from Galilee. During the years of His public ministry, these women had done much to provide for the material needs of the Lord and His Apostles. They had acted as mothers and sisters to them. Among these women were Mary Magdalen, Joanna, Susanna, Mary of Cleophas and Salome. Joanna was the wife of Chusa, who was a steward in the household of King Herod. Mary of Cleophas was the mother of James, Simon, Jude and Joseph. She seems to have been either the sister or sister-in-law (or perhaps a cousin) of the Blessed Virgin Mary. (See *John* 19:25). Because of this relationship, her sons were referred to as the brethren of Christ. Of Susanna, we know nothing except the name. Salome was the wife of Zebedee and the mother of the Apostles James and John. Mary Magdalen is well-known as the one who had turned from a life of sin to follow Christ.

These women of Galilee, and no doubt others whose names we do not know, were present on Calvary. The Gospels mention, besides St. John and the Blessed Virgin, just three others by name: Mary Magdalen, Mary of Cleophas and Salome. Thus, including the Blessed Mother, there were present at the crucifixion three Marys, John, and his mother, Salome. Besides these were the others whose names are not explicitly mentioned. The Gospel merely says that many women were there, looking on from a distance, who had followed Jesus from Galilee.

When the words "looking on afar off" (*Mark* 15:40) are used, it means most likely that the women stood in different groups, some at a distance, others right at the foot of the Cross, looking on the scene of the Crucifixion. Perhaps those at the foot of the Cross were originally at a distance and had gradually forced their way closer, by repeated returns, after the soldiers had tried to keep them away. Or maybe Our Lord's Mother and a few companions were allowed to stand close, and all the other women had to stand more at a distance.

They Suffer with Christ

To these devoted souls who so loved Jesus, it was a dreadful time. It is hard to see a loved one suffer.

It was especially hard to see Christ suffer because those who loved Him knew His unfailing goodness and kindness. They knew how much He had done for everybody, and very likely for most of *them,* curing bodily and spiritual ills. They knew His absolute innocence; they knew He suffered because of the malice of bitter enemies. To see someone suffer the pains of sickness is one thing. To see someone suffer public, shameful execution is another.

The bitter disgrace of their Master swept over the souls of the devoted women and filled to overflowing the cup of their sorrow. Those who loved more fully felt more deeply. Each of the women, according to the measure of her love and understanding, suffered along with Christ. It is characteristic of a good woman to enjoy to the full the successes of those she loves. It is likewise the price of her goodness that she feels acutely the failure and disgrace of those she loves. Since there was no more inglorious way to die than by crucifixion, the sorrow of these loving souls must have been extreme.

At this time there was nothing they could do but endure the sorrow. No soothing attentions were allowed. But later, when the body of Jesus was taken down from the Cross and hurriedly wrapped in linen and spices, the women of Galilee watched. Joseph of Arimathea and Nicodemus attended to the burial, but the women were not satisfied.

They Rejoice with Christ

On Saturday evening, the Sabbath being over at sundown, the women were able to shop for the additional spices they needed. Early on Sunday morning, as the sun was just beginning to lighten the eastern sky, Mary Magdalen and others of the group came hurrying to the sepulcher. They wondered about the heavy stone. In their haste and eagerness they had gone out so early, without summoning any of the men, that they thought of the heavy stone only as they were on the way. Of course, when they arrived, the sepulcher was empty. Christ had risen.

The Resurrection of Christ is today an accepted fact of history. Perhaps it even seems commonplace to us. But to these women who came to prepare the body properly for burial, probably reviewing in sorrowing conversation the terrible scenes of Friday, their immediate reaction at the tomb was astonishment. (*Lk.* 24:4). For instead of listening to one another's laments, they now heard an Angel in dazzling garments tell them: "Fear not you; for I know that you seek Jesus who was crucified. He is not here, for he is risen, as he said." (*Matt.* 28:5-6).

With the best news the world ever had, and with an Angel's injunction to tell it, the women were so taken aback that at first they would not say anything at all. "But they going out, fled from the sepulchre. For a trembling and fear had seized them: and they said nothing to any man;

for they were afraid." (*Mark* 16:8). But soon Our Lord Himself appeared to them. "And behold Jesus met them, saying: All hail. But they came up and took hold of his feet, and adored him. Then Jesus said to them: Fear not. Go, tell my brethren that they go into Galilee, there they shall see me." (*Matt.* 28:9-10). Reassured and eager, they then ran to tell the Apostles, who with manly disdain refused to believe them.

Devoted Women of Today

Throughout the world today there are other devoted women who minister to Christ, who weep over Him, who share His sorrows and His triumphs.

These women of today may be the mothers of families. In each of their children, they see first of all the soul won by the Blood of Christ. Their main joy is to see their children lead lives based on the teachings of His Church. These mothers are content when they see their children often receiving the Sacraments because they know that in this union with Christ, they are living in grace and growing more like their Lord. These mothers sorrow when they see Our Lord crucified again by the sins of the world. They grieve deeply if one of their own flesh and blood turns aside to mock the Saviour by disobeying the commandments of God or the Church. How many such good mothers are grieving today over sons and daughters who have driven the grace of Jesus Christ from their souls by unlawful and invalid marriages. Truly these women are also devoted women. They share Our Lord's joys and His sorrows.

There are others, too, unmarried, who have given their lives to the service of the Church in many ways. They press a cloth to the face of the suffering to soothe and to cleanse. They are wiping the face of Christ. They write or they teach to bring little children to the blessing of Christ. Perhaps they look after those who take Christ's place, His priests. Perhaps they care for the beauty of His dwelling place, the church; perhaps they work in the private charity of caring for an aged father or mother, or in the public charity of an organization. They too are devoted women who serve Our Lord; they share His triumphs and His sorrows.

Select Group

Our minds turn naturally to that consecrated group who, by solemn promises to God, have pledged themselves to lifelong and exclusive attending to the needs of Our Lord. These are the nuns. These especially are the daughters of Jerusalem and the women of Galilee. No others deserve these titles more. In schools, they spend their days trying to stamp the mind and heart of Christ on the souls of children. In hospitals and homes for the unfortunate, they bind up the wounds of Christ, whom they see in every man. As they look at the crucifixes in their chapels, as they make the Stations of the Cross, they walk in spirit over the way of the Cross and stand at the summit of Calvary's hill.

To fathers and mothers especially, one thought should be clear. If their daughters had wanted to serve Christ when He walked the earth, if their daughters had wanted to stand at the Cross, good parents would have rejoiced. Today they will rejoice also if their daughters wish to join the select group of devoted women who serve Christ in the religious life.

For all these devoted women of today, the mothers, the single, the consecrated, we are glad and give thanks. We are happy that in the midst of a world that still mocks and crucifies Christ, there are some who weep and sorrow with Him and attend to His needs.

～ 8 ～

MARY, THE MOTHER OF OUR LORD

WHEN we think of Christ dying on the Cross, a very important part of the picture is His mother standing beneath it. She stands there, a silent, heroic figure. No other action of hers, no word on that day has been recorded in Sacred Scripture. The deep drama of what she thought and felt seems at first glance to be hidden completely. Yet if we keep looking and searching, the haze lifts. The drama is open and present and alive to us because we do know Mary, the Mother of Our Lord.

The Apostles were taken by surprise when Our Lord was arrested. Their surprise grew and changed into terror when He was condemned to death. Their world crashed when He was nailed to the Cross and actually died a criminal's death. Their reaction may seem strange, since Christ had definitely and clearly foretold His sufferings and death. At the third prediction, He had said plainly regarding Himself: "For he shall be delivered to the Gentiles, and shall be mocked, and scourged, and spit upon: and after they have scourged him, they will put him to death." (*Luke* 18:32-33).

77

Mary Not Surprised

Our Lord's Mother, however, was not surprised. She had not dismissed these words so
lightly. Instead, they spelled out for her in shocking detail and with a sense of sudden nearness
what she had known for many years. She had
never forgotten the words of Simeon in the Temple: "Behold this child is set for the fall, and for
the resurrection of many in Israel, and for a sign
which shall be contradicted; and thy own soul a
sword shall pierce, that, out of many hearts,
thoughts may be revealed." (*Luke* 2:34-35). Mary
had pondered the words of Isaias: "He shall be
led as a sheep to the slaughter, and shall be
dumb as a lamb before his shearer, and he shall
not open his mouth." (*Is.* 53:7).

Mary was not surprised. She did not know the
sudden terror of looking at unexpected tragedy.
But she did feel the icy grip of a reality long
expected. All of us know that our parents or our
dear friends suffering from a fatal illness must
soon die. But that does not lessen the force of sorrow when the reality of suffering and death is
present. Mary on Good Friday was the mother
who had been expecting a son's death. It was
something like the mother who watches over a
child wasting away with an incurable disease. Yet
it was different, too, because her Son had just
been in perfect health. It was different and
deeper because of the added elements of disgrace
and violence. It was different and deeper because
of the purity and strength of her love for Him.

She Prays and She Suffers

Because of His human will, Our Lord cried out in agony: "Father, if thou wilt, remove this chalice from me." (*Luke* 22:42). He did this despite His own prophecies and His sure knowledge of their fulfillment. Mary's own knowledge was not so sure nor so complete. Perhaps she would hope against hope that the prophecies were, in part at least, symbolic.

We do not know just where Our Lady spent the night of Holy Thursday. Yet it seems reasonable to suppose that she too made the strongest and most piteous plea that ever reached the ear of Almighty God: Father, if it be possible, remove this cup from Him.

At the same time, she who once had said, "Behold the handmaid of the Lord," now bowed her head in acceptance and echoed the words of her Son: "Not my will, but Thine be done." From the beginning to the bitter end, she was always the *Ancilla Domini,* the handmaid of the Lord. But we must never forget that her *fiat* now was throbbingly alive, a deep response to maternal love.

So, in a sense, the events of Good Friday did develop step by step in shocking newness before the eyes of Mary. The Blood of Christ flowed down His body, spurted from His hands and feet and head and Mary saw its fresh redness. As it mixed with the dust in the street and the trampled earth of Calvary, the smothering sorrow grew within her. It was as though the dust mixed with her own blood and made heavy her whole being. Saintly mystics have said that so close was the harmony of spirit between Mary and her Son that she suffered everything He suffered. In the Litany of Loreto we invoke her as "Queen of Martyrs."

Through the years, Our Lady had perhaps pictured these things. Her knowledge of the ancient prophecies and the special prophecy of Simeon would naturally lead her to do this. The more recent prediction of her Son, that He was to suffer and die by crucifixion (*Matt.* 20:19), would have renewed all those pictures from her long years of meditation. Reluctantly, she had to relinquish any hopes that Our Lord's suffering might not be too severe. From her reflection on the lowly and trying circumstances of His birth and early life, she knew that God did not spare His own. Yet, as the drama now unfolded on Good Friday, it was real and it was new.

Mary in Scripture

It has often been said that there are many things we would like to know about Mary, the Mother of Jesus, which we do not know. The Gospel writers are very sparing in their descriptions. St. Mark introduces Our Lord as a grown man at His Baptism. St. John dwells sublimely on the Word made flesh, and then he likewise proceeds to the Baptism of Christ. St. Matthew tells us of the birth of the Baby Jesus, the coming of the Magi, the flight into Egypt and the return to Nazareth. St. Luke is the most complete, giving us the story of the Annunciation, the Visitation, the Nativity, the shepherds at the crib, the Presentation in the Temple and the Finding of the Child in the Temple.

During the public life of Christ, Mary appears just four times. St. John relates the account of the wedding feast at Cana. The other three Evangelists tell of the incident in which Our Lord was told that His mother and brethren were waiting to see Him. He answered, "My mother and my brethren are they who hear the word of God, and do it." (*Luke* 8:21). Only St. Luke records the praise of the woman in the crowd for the mother of Him who was speaking. Our Lord again used this incident to make a point in His teaching: "Blessed are they who hear the word of God and keep it." (*Luke* 11:28). The fourth and final time we meet the Blessed Virgin Mary during the Public Life of Jesus is at the foot of the Cross. (*John* 19:25-27). (The *Acts of the Apostles* tell us that she was present with the others at the coming of the Holy Ghost on Pentecost Sunday.)

The Scripture writers had their task to do, and they fulfilled it. They intended no more neglect of Mary than they did of Our Lord when His years from twelve to thirty are passed over in one sentence. No more neglect is present than when St. John simply dismisses some of the world's greatest events by saying: "But there are also many other things which Jesus did; which, if they were written every one, the world itself, I think, would not be able to contain the books that should be written." (*John* 21:25).

Early Traditions

In the early days of Christianity, the staggering task of converting the pagan world consumed the Apostles and their co-workers. If anyone wanted to know more details about the life of Christ and His Mother, they could go to His living friends and relatives, who could supply the information. But after a while, Christians wanted to treasure up and preserve more of the details regarding the lives of Jesus and Mary.

So, between the second and seventh centuries various traditions were written down. Many apocryphal books were composed—that is, books which the Church decided were not part of authentic Scripture, such as the "gospel of James." These give many additional details about Our Lord and His Mother beyond what we know from Sacred Scripture: the ox and the ass at the crib, the names of Mary's parents, the names of the Magi, their title of kings, the presentation of Mary in the Temple—all have their origin in the apocrypha. No doubt much of the content is true, and represents constant historical traditions. But the Church does not include these stories among the teachings that the faithful must believe, since human traditions may be either true or false. However, the Church also has *divine* Tradition, which she recognizes as equal in authority to Sacred Scripture and which we are obliged to believe.

The Church Is Our Guide

The Church, of course, is the living voice of Christ. The Catholic Church has and will continue to unfold the beautiful petals of truth about Mary that have always been present. The Church is the sure guide in telling us of the Immaculate Conception, the Divine Maternity, the Assumption, the position of Mary as Mediatrix of graces. These truths were always present in the Deposit of Faith, but became more clearly and definitely seen as time went on. This is the process, not of making things up, but of discovering more and more about what one already possesses, like a student seeing more and more in a great poem as he rereads it.

The Gospels present a limited number of facts. The apocrypha give a few more details, which must be carefully sorted out. The Church gives us the essential and deep doctrinal truths. From these elements, we can build up an acquaintance with the Blessed Virgin Mary that is remarkably sure and complete.

We can, if we wish, come to know her better than we know many of our relatives and friends. We can know her better than we know the women of history, about whom a comparitive infinitude of details has been preserved. We can come to know her better than we know those women who sat for portraits by great artists, or whose features have been captured by the camera.

We Do Know the Real Mary

When do we really know a person? The answer to that holds the key to our knowledge of the Mother of Jesus. We know a person, not when we know the weight, the height, the color of the hair and eyes, the vivacity of manner, the features of the face. All these can tell us only something *about* the real person. The real person is inside, captured by, and only to some degree revealed by, the body. The real person is in the thoughts, the emotions, the will. If you know these, then you know the person.

You do not yet really know a person when you know his date of birth, schools attended, adventures gone through, successes attained. These again are merely indications of how the real, essential person acted. They may be interesting details and stories. But one must analyze all of them together to know the person. If, however, one knows one tremendous fact about a person, such as Mary's Divine Motherhood, he needs no analysis. This immediately puts him, according to his own degree of comprehension of the essential fact, within the thoughts, the emotions and the will of Mary.

We often know many facts about an individual, and yet are much surprised by the way he turns out. Very often, this phenomenon is owed to knowing just facts, and not really knowing the person. On the other hand, it is possible, and this is the case with the Blessed Mother, to know few facts and yet know her very well through faith, prayer and devotion.

Christian piety has tried to demonstrate some understanding of the essential truths about Mary by giving her numerous titles, such as those set forth in her litany. No one name is enough for her, no matter how beautiful. One who loves another closely usually finds nicknames to capture the spirit, the mood, the beauty, the uniqueness of the one loved. In like manner, those who have loved Mary through the centuries have found many names to try to show the essence of her person, which has overwhelmed their understanding.

Because She Was Chosen

One of the tricks of suspense in a movie is to show someone under an umbrella or hat. Suddenly the face appears, and immediately you recognize the person. It takes only a small area to make the identification sure, if that area is essential. So it is enough if we just see the "face" of Mary, meaning her inner soul. In her case, that soul was full of grace and of the dignity of Divine Motherhood. Knowing this, we realize that her essential cast of mind, the truest part of her was always turned to God. Knowing that He chose her, we know that all the good we see in any woman was in her.

We Know Her from Her Words

The truest acquaintance with any person is to know the thoughts that stir the will, which is the root of the emotions. The words that one speaks are the surest ordinary index of what one thinks and feels. This is especially true of the words spoken at a time of crisis or importance, when we reach deep within ourselves to call forth the best possible answer.

Not many words of Mary are recorded. St. Luke tells us what she said on three occasions: at the Annunciation, at the Visitation, and at the Finding of the Child in the Temple. St. John preserves her simple statement and command at the wedding feast: "They have no wine," and "Whatsoever he shall say to you, do ye." (*John* 2:3, 5).

When the Angel Gabriel brought his message, Mary had one question: "How shall this be done, because I know not man?" (*Luke* 1:34). After listening to the reply, she gave simple, unqualified consent: "Behold the handmaid of the Lord; be it done to me according to thy word." Years later, after she and St. Joseph had sought Jesus for three days, she poured forth a mother's pent-up anguish by saying: "Son, why hast thou done so to us? Behold thy father and I have sought thee sorrowing." Our Lady's only discourse of any length is the *Magnificat,* and this is a hymn of praise to God.

We can be happy that these few instances of the Blessed Mother's speaking have been preserved. For they show us a definite pattern of thought and feeling. They show us that Mary was alert to the Will of God and the needs of man. They show her alive to ordinary emotions, capable of being hurt, not having all her problems immediately solved by overwhelming grace. They show a person empty of selfishness, but full of the wonder of God's goodness, wisdom and power.

Pondering in Her Heart

It is of significance, too, that though so few of her words are preserved, St. Luke should refer three times to her habit of thoughtful reflection. At the Angel's greeting, she "thought with herself what manner of salutation this should be." (*Luke* 1:29). After the shepherds left the crib, "Mary kept all these words, pondering *them* in her heart." (*Luke* 2:19). Later, after telling of the finding of Jesus, St. Luke again says that: "His mother kept all these words in her heart." (*Luke* 2:51).

There have been thousands of books written about the events in Christ's life. Men have studied and reflected. They have interpreted the minutest details, sometimes coming to differing conclusions. Mary also pondered all the details, which she knew at firsthand. She had a great start on the best scholars, for she was an eyewitness. But still she thought and reflected, trying to see more and more into God's wonderful plans. Books have been composed on the Our Father, on the Beatitudes, on the Parables. Every word that Christ spoke in the

Gospels has been treasured and made the subject of thousands of sermons. Mary, too, remembered and reflected on all these, and surely on many others that we have never heard.

Her philosophy, her way of thinking, her cast of mind, the roots of her emotions sprang from Christ, from the events that surrounded Him and from the words that He spoke. Her thoughts were very much like those of Christ. She was the woman who pondered, who reflected. She kept things carefully in her heart.

The insights of Mary, so alive to grace, so totally wrapped up in Christ, must have been unsurpassable. But even for her, there was always the possibility of growing in understanding. Even for her, there was necessary that leap beyond understanding into the realm of pure faith. Then with the added light of this faith, she pondered yet more.

Thus, to know Mary is to know what she kept so carefully in her heart. To know her is to go over the events of Christ's life, to listen to the words He said, to study these in the light of faith and of reason.

There are clever, trick pictures which show both the face of Jesus and of Mary. You look at the picture and see Our Lord, and then you see the face of Mary. The reality is no trick. When you look at Our Lord, you see His Mother. When you know Him, you know her. When you look at her, you see Him. If you try to keep them completely apart, you will tear up the image of both.

Mary's Sacrifice

On Good Friday, we have Jesus and Mary together. He was nailed to the Cross. She stood beneath it. He spoke His last words. She listened; again she stored up these words, so sharply and indelibly imprinted on her memory. While He suffered the indignity and the pain in mind and body, she suffered it all in her heart. Christ's Will was perfectly turned to God. His sacrifice was intense and complete because it had taken supreme effort to conform His human will to His Father's divine Will. We can be sure that Mary's whole being had cried out at the suffering and insult to her Son. Her offering, too, was intense and complete because it was made with supreme effort.

"It was she, the second Eve, who, free from all sin, Original or personal, and always most intimately united with her Son, offered Him on Golgotha to the Eternal Father for all the children of Adam, sin-stained by his unhappy fall, and her mother's rights and mother's love were included in the holocaust." (Pius XII in *Mystici Corporis*).

According to the traditions of Christian art, Mary received the body of her Son into her arms when Joseph of Arimathea and Nicodemus took it down from the Cross. Scripture and art are both silent on her thoughts and actions in the interval between Christ's death and this tender scene. For one thing, she had witnessed the thrust of the spear that opened Our Lord's side, and she had seen the blood and water come forth. The lifeless

body received the spear silently, without move-
ment. But a shudder must have shaken the
Mother. She had seen horror and pain and degra-
dation piled one upon the other. At this time she
was not sure what would happen to the body of
Jesus. More indignity might be heaped upon it.
Perhaps it would be thrown into a common grave.
As Our Lord had died with two thieves, He might
be buried with them. There was no strict right
recognized in claiming the body of one who had
died a criminal's death.

When Joseph and Nicodemus obtained permission from Pilate to bury Christ, Mary was surely
much relieved. Her Son was at least to have a
decent burial. So Mary, for a few moments, held
the lifeless body. She watched the swift preparations, thankful for the thoughtfulness that provided the spices and the linen. She followed
Joseph and Nicodemus to the tomb and looked at
the heavy stone. Its weight was as nothing compared to the weight of sorrow that oppressed her.
Then she took the guiding hand of St. John and
followed him to the house where he led her.

Mary Close to Us All

We do not know many of the details about the
Mother of Christ. We do not know many things
that would be comforting and interesting. But we
do know the Blessed Mother better than any
woman of all history. For we see her in the scenes
dearest to a Christian, the scene of the infancy of

Jesus, the scene of His death. We know her in her inmost thoughts and desires, which were the thoughts and desires of Christ. We know her in her inmost person because she was full of grace and was the Mother of God.

Our surest knowledge of the Mother of Jesus does not come through a long, circuitous route. It springs straight from the knowledge that comes from faith and love. It grows as we grow—in the knowledge of all the truths and the history of Christianity. Poets, writers and artists have been inspired by her. They knew her so well that all the reality they held in their minds could never be satisfactorily reproduced in words, picture or statue.

Through the centuries and still today, men speak her name with familiarity and ease: Our Lady, the Blessed Virgin, Our Mother, or just Mary. Even a young child can kneel down and speak to her in close intimacy. That is perhaps the best proof that Mary is the best known and most loved woman of history.

～ 9 ～

HEROD ANTIPAS

IN the early morning of Good Friday, two men stood face to face. One was a puppet king, the tetrarch of Galilee and Peraea, who did not by right have the title or the power of king. The other was He who could claim kingship over Heaven and earth. The puppet king was arrayed in the robes of state, surrounded by courtiers and servants. The real King was surrounded by armed guards and outspoken enemies. The puppet king, officially the tetrarch, was selfish and sinful. The real King was ready to give up His spotless life for the sins of men. The name of the one was Herod Antipas; the other was Jesus Christ.

The reason Christ now stood before Herod was that Pontius Pilate, the Roman governor of Judea, Idumea and Samaria did not want to make a judgment against his conscience. Pilate knew that Jesus was innocent, and when he heard that He was from Galilee, he immediately sent Him to Herod. (*Luke* 23:7). Herod Antipas was in Jerusalem at the time because it was the eve of the great feast day of the Pasch. Therefore, the journey from the court of Pilate to that of Herod was not long.

According to Roman law, a man could be tried

in the place a crime was committed, or he could be tried by the authorities of the district he came from. According to this arrangement, for instance, a resident of Missouri who committed a crime in Indiana could be sent back to Missouri for judgment. This sending of Jesus from Pilate to Herod is history's most famous exemplification of "passing the buck."

Herod's Long Reign

The man Christ now stood before had been the ruler of Galilee all the time He had lived there. When Joseph brought the Child and His mother back from Egypt, he feared to go back to Judea, which was under Archelaus, but went instead up to Nazareth, which was in Galilee. Therefore, one point we can mention favorably about Herod Antipas is that Joseph judged his half-brother, Archelaus, more dangerous. So Christ had lived almost His entire life under the government of Herod Antipas. Most of His public life too, His preaching and instructing, had been done in the territory of this man. But this was their first meeting, on the morning of Good Friday.

The Herod of Good Friday is not, however, the Herod who tried to kill Christ as an infant. The Herod of Christ's early infancy is known to history as Herod the Great. He was the father of Herod Antipas. Herod the Great was an Idumean by birth and had curried Roman favor until he was made the king over all of Palestine. His character may be judged by what he did in trying to kill the Infant Jesus. He had all the boys who lived in Bethlehem and its neighborhood, and who were two years old or under, put to death. Of course, this was nothing for one who had killed his wife, his mother-in-law, brother-in-law, and three of his sons, and who had begun his reign by dispatching 45 members of the Jewish Sanhedrin. In earlier days, this Council had brought him to trial for murder, and Herod resented the idea. This was Herod the Great, father of the man before whom Christ stood on Good Friday. To put it mildly, Herod Antipas did not come from a good family background. Neither had he had a good religious training. He had spent most of his youth in Rome, where he picked up the pagan, Hellenistic culture of the time.

Herod Antipas, the Herod of Christ's public life, the Herod of Good Friday, received his kingdom on the death of his father. At that time, the larger kingdom was divided by order of Caesar Augustus into three parts among the three sons of Herod the Great. Besides Antipas, there were Herod Philip and Archelaus.

Took the Wife of Half-Brother

Herod Antipas had married the daughter of Aretas, a king of Arabia. But when he went to Rome later, he became infatuated with Herodias, the wife of his half-brother, Philip, who lived as a private citizen there. Since their father, Herod the Great, had married at least ten times, there were many half-brothers. Herodias left Philip and went to live with Herod, while his real wife fled back to her father.

St. John the Baptist, the stalwart proclaimer of truth, did not mince words. He said to Herod Antipas: "It is not lawful for thee to have thy brother's wife." (*Mark* 6:18). In saying this, he incurred the enmity of Herodias. She did not rest until John had been put into prison. She did not, in fact, rest then, but schemed ways and means of getting John put to death. Herod Antipas knew John was a just and good man. Perhaps as the historian Josephus says, Herod feared John's influence with the people. But he also liked to hear John speak, and though he had put him into prison, he protected John from further harm. But a scheming, hate-filled woman will find a way. Herodias found hers.

Made Rash Promise

At her unlawful husband's birthday party, she had her daughter Salome, child of her own real husband, come in and dance. This was a novelty to Herod and the guests, who were accustomed to professional entertainers. The dance need not have been so sensual that it made Herod lose his wits. The Gospel of St. Mark says that she "pleased Herod, and them that were at table with him." (*Mark* 6:22). He simply felt obliged to do something for this special performance, and likewise he wanted to show his expansiveness and magnanimity before his guests. So Herod made a grand promise. "Ask of me what thou wilt, and I will give it to thee." (*Mark* 6:22). And he swore he would give whatever was asked, even half his kingdom.

The plot was well laid. Instructed by her evil mother, Herodias, the daughter asked for the head of John the Baptist on a plate. Not willing to go back on the oath taken before his guests, Herod had this gruesome and murderous request granted. John the Baptist died because of speaking the truth, because of a woman's hate, and because of a man's weakness.

Herod Worries

Later on, Herod Antipas worried about this deed. As Christ became well known through His miracles, Herod came to hear of Him. He worried that perhaps John the Baptist had risen from the dead and that this was now he working the miracles. However, he was not sure. At one time he kept repeating, "John the Baptist is risen again from the dead, and therefore mighty works shew forth themselves in him." (*Mark* 6:14). With a guilty conscience he said: "John whom I beheaded, he is risen again from the dead." (*Mark* 6:16). At another time he was perplexed and asked: "John I have beheaded; but who is this of whom I hear such things?" (*Luke* 9:9).

Herod was afraid to lay hands on Jesus, but he wished that He would go away. So he used the

Pharisees to try to trick Our Lord into getting out of Galilee. They went at his instructions and told Jesus: "Depart, and get thee hence, for Herod hath a mind to kill thee." (*Luke* 13:31). Our Lord naturally saw through this pretense and responded by calling Herod a fox. "Go and tell that fox, Behold, I cast out devils, and do cures to day and to morrow, and the third day I am consummated." (*Luke* 13:32). Jesus meant to leave on the third day, but in the meantime, He would just ignore Herod.

By Good Friday morning, Herod Antipas must have recovered from much of his fright, for when Pilate's messenger came announcing the coming of Our Lord, Herod was very glad. Now he had a chance to see Jesus, and in the present circumstances he flattered himself that Jesus might work a miracle right before him.

He asked Our Lord many questions. Perhaps he promised release if a miracle were worked. At any rate the chief priests and scribes standing nearby were violently alarmed. They were afraid that Herod might release Jesus, so they kept accusing Him. Herod paid no attention to them, but continued to ask Jesus many questions.

No Answer for Insincerity

To all of Herod's questions, Jesus gave no answer. He would not answer because there was no sincere seeking after anything worthwhile in all the questions. Herod was not trying to establish guilt or lack of guilt. He was just trying to satisfy his own idle curiosity. He did not ask anything sincerely about his own soul's welfare. Therefore, Our Lord would have nothing to say. Here was the greatest opportunity that this ambitious, petty king ever had. "What good shall I do that I may have life everlasting?" he might have asked, as had the rich young man. (*Matt.* 19:16). But he asked no question with a serious purpose, either in reference to himself or to Our Lord. Therefore, he received no answer.

The silence of Our Lord shouted more loudly than any words in condemnation of Herod. Herod's foolish questions betrayed weakness. Christ's silence showed strength. And Herod felt this. He knew that despite his position of authority and his regal robes, he was the man on the spot; and the Prisoner in stained garments, saying nothing, was the master of the situation.

Mockery

Herod took the weakling's way of regaining his own dignity before others. He mocked Christ and tried to make Him look like a fool. "Herod with his army set him at nought, and mocked him, putting on him a white garment . . ." (*Luke* 23:11). It is easy to imagine Herod saying: "Oh, you are too important to reply to the questions of your king! In fact, you claim to be a king. Very well. We will bow to you. Bring in the kingly robe." Our Lord was clothed with the fine, shining garment. Herod and his soldiers then had their fun. They outdid one another in their coarse jokes.

In the art of mockery, it is customary to use the expressions of the one mocked, but to twist their meaning. It is customary to give ridiculous interpretations to the deeds of the one mocked. So we can well imagine how Our Lord's good works and miracles and sublime words were twisted about by this early-morning display of wit. Of His silence, they might have said: "He didn't work a miracle on the deaf and dumb man. He gave him His own tongue." Of His refusal to show some sign: "He knows He can't fool a court."

Friends Again

The fun over, Herod sent the Prisoner back to Pilate. These two leaders became friends again. Most likely, Pontius Pilate had angered Herod by killing some Galileans, subjects of Herod, who were taking part in a riot. The estrangement was broken on Good Friday because Pilate's act in sending Jesus to Herod flattered the latter. (Cf. *Luke* 23:12).

Thus the interlude with Herod ended. The only visible "good" result was that Pilate and Herod again became friends. But there is a strong lesson to be learned in considering the relationship of Herod and Jesus.

Sensuality and Blindness

The lesson is summed up thus: The sensual man does not perceive the things that are of the

Spirit of God. Sensuality leads to spiritual blindness. Herod was a sensual man. He proved that by stealing his brother's wife and keeping her in defiance of God's law and the general opinion of the Jews. Herod knew of Our Lord's miracles. He had, in fact, worried about them, afraid that Jesus was John the Baptist risen from the dead. Yet the miracles made no salutary impression on him. He apparently never asked himself whether or not this proved the hand of God was present, never asked himself what he personally should do. When Jesus Christ stood before him on Good Friday and he had the opportunity to ask serious questions, he did not. He wanted a miracle. If Our Lord had worked a miracle, it would not have benefited his soul. None of the other miracles had, which he already knew of. Herod was spiritually blind because he was sensual. He could see only his own wants and planned to satisfy his own desires.

Jesus had once advised His Apostles: "Take heed and beware of the leaven of the Pharisees, and of the leaven of Herod." (*Mark* 8:15). This meant: beware of their moral corruption. Immediately after this, He said, as they argued about not having any bread: "Do you not yet know nor understand? Have you still your heart blinded?" (*Mark* 8:17). He then explained about how they had seen the miracles of the multiplication of the loaves and fishes, yet still did not have confidence in Him. It is significant that when speaking of blindness, Our Lord warned against the leaven of

Herod. This indicated that Herod's corruption had blinded him.

Some very great miracles have been worked in our century. We think of Lourdes with its well-authenticated cases—for instance, the severely mentally handicapped, paralyzed boy cured instantly on being bathed in the water. We think of the miracle of the sun at Fatima on October 13, 1917, seen by 70,000 at one time. We think of the cases accepted by the Church in the processes of beatification and canonization of her Saints, all carefully documented. Yet the impression they make on a sensual generation is light and passing.

Impurity and Crime

A second conclusion is that unfaithfulness in matters of sexual morality easily leads to other crimes. It is fashionable to picture the easily divorced, the impure, as hurting only themselves. That is false. In order to satisfy sinful desires, in order to get just what he wants, the impure person will walk over the rights of others. Such persons make havoc with the lives of children and do not hesitate to destroy the happiness of another's husband or wife by shoving them out. Sometimes murder and suicide result. Herod's impurity led to the death of the man of whom Our Lord had said that none greater had been born of woman. (Cf. *Matt.* 11:11.) John the Baptist, greater than any of the prophets, lost his head because he rebuked the impurity of Herod and Herodias.

Sin Is Joyless

A third conclusion can be drawn from a consideration of the life of Herod Antipas. Sin brings with it its own punishment. Herod killed John and afterward suffered over it. He became worried and uneasy. Herod, likewise, suffered by spending his life with Herodias. Though he was infatuated with her, she must often have caused him grief by her selfishness. It seems that there were no complaints from the half-brother, Philip, from whom Herod had stolen her. A woman hateful enough to have a man killed and his head brought into a birthday banquet must certainly have often been a selfish, unpleasant companion in marriage. She egged Herod on to a war with Aretas IV, his father-in-law. Finally, he lost his kingdom because of Herodias. She persuaded him to go to Rome to obtain the royal title. His own brother, however, Agrippa I, arranged a charge of treason against Herod Antipas, which was waiting for him when he arrived in Rome. Herod and Herodias were sent into exile in France. He died, not a king or even a tetrarch, but deposed, a private citizen in a foreign land.

On Good Friday, Herod Antipas had Jesus before him. But Jesus spoke to him not a word. Herod, because of his insincerity, did not merit a reply. And he was insincere because he was blinded by his sensuality. He could not perceive the things that were of the Spirit of God. We must, therefore, beware of the leaven of Herod, beware of sensuality and impurity. For it leads to spiritual blindness, to insincerity in things that really count. Sometimes it leads to a complete loss of faith. Whether the blindness is complete or not, the spiritual vision is always dimmed by sensuality. We should remember the words of Our Lord: "Blessed are the clean in heart: for they shall see God." (*Matt.* 5:8).

∽ 10 ∽

PONTIUS PILATE

FROM A.D. 6 to A.D. 41, the part of Palestine included in Judea, Idumea and Samaria was ruled by a succession of seven Roman governors. Only a scholar could tell you the names of six of them. The other man's name is known to hundreds of millions of people. Most of us have learned it and pronounced it as we recited our prayers thousands of times. Millions today will say the name of the most famous governor in history as they recite the Apostles' Creed: "suffered under Pontius Pilate."

Pontius Pilate was the Roman governor or procurator of Judea for about ten years, from circa 26-36 A.D. He was fifth in the line of the seven governors. Before them had been Herod the Great, who ruled all of Palestine, and Archelaus, Herod's son who had inherited just the third part, that part which soon went to the Roman procurators by order of Augustus. After them came Herod Agrippa I, for just three short years, then another succession of Roman governors.

Background

Pilate had had his troubles with the Jews. He was not fond of them, nor were they fond of him. On one occasion, there had been a riot in which some Galileans were killed. This riot may have been occasioned by Pilate's using some of the Temple funds to build an aqueduct to improve the Jerusalem water supply. Once, too, Pilate had excited strong opposition by putting up standards with the image of Tiberius. He had also once been ordered by the Emperor to put away some gilt shields that he had set up over the protest of the people.

The territory governed by the Roman procurator was at most 90 miles in length and 50 miles in width. His powers of ruling were broad, but he was an appointee of the Roman Emperor and could be removed at will.

Ordinarily, Pilate lived at Caesarea in the palace built by Herod the Great. But at the time of the big feast days, when there was a large gathering in Jerusalem, he came down with some of his cohort of soldiers. There were about 3,000 in the full group. In this way he could keep order, prevent any outbreaks by a show of force, and quickly quell riots and disturbances.

Pilate was in Jerusalem on Good Friday because the city was crowded, as preparations went on for the celebration of the solemn Feast of the Jewish Pasch. He stayed at such times in the Fortress Antonia, a castle abutting on the northwest corner of the Temple enclosure. This had also been built by Herod the Great. It seems quite sure that Pilate was staying at the Fortress Antonia on Good Friday and that this, therefore, was the location of the trial of Christ.

Nothing definite is known of Pilate's previous life or his family background. Some have surmised that he was a freedman who rose from the ranks. To be a governor, he would have to be of the equestrian rank.

Character

Pilate was a man of some talent and cleverness. His quick and clear perception of Christ's innocence, his ingenuity at devising ways of trying to save Him, show this. The fact that Pilate was a Roman governor says something for him; the fact that he kept his job for ten years in a territory rebellious and hard-to-handle says more. It has been said that he was cruel and obstinate. His conduct on Good Friday does not show that. Rather, it shows a man trying to procure justice, but weak enough in principle and character to allow cruelty and injustice to have their way. On Good Friday, he was not the bitter prosecutor, nor even the unfeeling, insensitive man who laughed off the life of another. He was the lawyer for the defense; but he allowed himself to be pushed back from compromise to compromise until he finally passed the most unjust sentence in history.

Pilate had given to the Jews the choice of Christ

or Barabbas. They finally maneuvered *him* into the situation where he had to choose between Jesus and Pilate. He chose to protect his own skin from possible damage rather than continue to defend Our Lord.

History's most famous governor began history's most famous trial early in the morning. The Jewish Sanhedrin had met at dawn to confirm the sentence passed during the night. This was to make it legal. Then, since they did not have the power of actually executing the sentence of death, they hastened to see the governor, who did possess this power. No doubt a messenger had been sent on ahead to inform the governor that the Sanhedrin were coming with a prisoner on whom the death penalty had been decreed.

The Jews Wanted No New Trial

The Jewish leaders wanted Pontius Pilate to be a rubber stamp. He was supposed to sit down in the judgment seat and give the official sentence. But as he came out on Good Friday morning to meet the Jewish leaders—who would not enter his house for fear of legal defilement—he shocked the enemies of Our Lord by re-opening the case. "What accusation bring you against this man?" he asked. (*John* 18:29). The answer showed that all that was expected of the governor was to be a rubber stamp. They had already judged the prisoner. "If he were not a malefactor, we would not have delivered him up to thee." (*John* 18:30). Pilate turned this answer against them: "Take him you, and judge him according to your law." (*John* 18:31). In other words, if you are handling the case, why do you not just do the whole thing.

Pilate knew they were looking for a death sentence, and with this remark he wrung from them the humiliating admission: "It is not lawful for us to put any man to death." (*John* 18:31). No longer did the Jews govern themselves with supreme civil authority. The Romans reserved whatever rights they wished, and the passing of the sentence of death was one such right.

Three Charges

Seeing that a new case had to be made against Our Lord, the Jewish leaders brought forth three charges. These charges were sedition, antifiscal agitation, and pretension to royal sovereignty. "We have found this man perverting our nation, and forbidding to give tribute to Caesar, and saying that he is Christ the king." (*Luke* 23:2). Pontius Pilate apparently took notice only of the last charge. He must have noted the air of quiet authority and the calm, kingly dignity of the Prisoner. He knew this was no ordinary rabble-rouser, stirring up rebellion among the Jews and agitating against the payment of taxes. If He were anything, this man had kingly blood in Him.

Pilate Pursues One Charge

Pilate was interested in finding out something about the background of this Man. He asked directly: "Art thou the king of the Jews?" (*John* 18:33). Jesus answered: "Sayest thou this thing of thyself, or have others told it thee of me?" (*John* 18:34). Pilate was abashed that his own interest and his surmise of royal dignity had been perceived by this Prisoner, and he answered gruffly: "Am I a Jew? Thy own nation, and the chief priests, have delivered thee up to me: what hast thou done?" (*John* 18:35). Jesus ignored the last question and went back to answer the first. He explained that He indeed had a kingdom, but His kingdom was not of this world. Pilate wanted his own surmise definitely corroborated and asked again directly: "Art thou a king then?" (*John* 18:37). Jesus answered in the affirmative: "Thou sayest that I am a king. For this was I born, and for this came I into the world; that I should give testimony to the truth. Every one that is of the truth, heareth my voice." (*John* 18:37).

What Is Truth?

Then He made a statement that was an invitation to the governor. Jesus said that all who were of the truth heard His voice. But Pilate was not ready for such a grace. Instead of looking for instruction with an open mind and heart, he merely cast off the invitation by saying, "What is truth?" (*John* 18:38).

Pilate is the symbol of whole hosts of men who throughout the centuries and yet today close their minds against the truth. Christ stood before Pilate and extended an invitation to learn the truth. Pilate refused, and this first indifference to the truth soon led him from compromise to compromise, and finally to the condemnation and deliverance of Jesus to be crucified.

The Church stands before the world and issues the invitation to learn the truth. She claims she alone has the complete truth—and that unmixed with error. But how many shrug off the invitation, saying skeptically that it is impossible to find religious truth. Like Pilate, they are then led from compromise to compromise. In the end, they find themselves on the same side as the bitterest enemies of the Church. Though they may protest innocence, they follow in morals and doctrine the forces of Satan, and deliver Jesus Christ to be crucified. Pilate saw in Jesus only a man, though an extraordinary one. Today they see in the Church only a human organization, though a truly extraordinary one.

Today more than ever, Our Lord, through His Church, can make heard the claim to know the truth. Through radio, television, newspaper and magazine articles, and books, millions have the opportunity to hear definitely the claim: "For this was I born, and for this came I into the world; that I should give testimony to the truth. Every one that is of the truth, heareth my voice." (*John* 18:37).

The Knights of Columbus Religious Information Program in the U.S., during the period from its beginning in 1948 until October 31, 1961, had received 4,212,980 inquiries and requests; 439,879 people actually went further to enroll for the complete course. This is a remarkable achievement. But how many millions had shrugged off the invitation, had excused themselves from making any sincere effort to know the validity of the Church's claims to be the living voice of Christ! And how many untold millions go on the same today as these others—and as Pontius Pilate did, 2,000 years ago.

Yes, what is truth? Many organized religions parcel out only those parts of the truth they choose to hold, and they reject the rest. Those who walk on as rugged individualists formulate their own codes of dogma and morals. Thus, divorce and remarriage, contraception, immoral operations, "art" for art's sake, continue unchecked, uncurbed. Everybody claims innocence. The Sacraments given by Christ are neglected, discounted. The Blessed Mother is not given the honor due to her. Everyone today is presumed innocent of any wrongdoing—but Jesus Christ, God-made-Man, our Redeemer from the Original Sin of Adam and Eve, is delivered to be scourged and crucified.

Going outside again to the Jews gathered on the terrace, Pilate spoke a truth that he *did* perceive: "I find no cause in this man." (*Luke* 23:4). This was the first of at least four declarations of Christ's innocence by His Roman judge.

Pilate Sends Jesus to Herod

When the charges of sedition and many other charges (*Mark* 15:4) were repeated, Jesus answered not a word. This extraordinary silence in the face of dangerous accusations amazed Pilate. He was accustomed to see violence met with violence, angry accusations with angry denials. This stately, self-possessed silence stirred up in the soul of Pilate respect and perhaps even awe for the Prisoner. When he heard the name of Galilee mentioned, he seized upon it gladly and sent Jesus to Herod, the ruler of Galilee.

This was Pilate's first specific act of compromise. It was a negative act, a refusal to release immediately a person he was convinced was innocent. It was an evasion of responsibility, a failure to take positive measures to protect an innocent man.

Here again, the Roman governor shows the pattern usually followed by so many people who are inclined to good, but weak enough to sacrifice principle for convenience. Not willing to encounter open opposition, they evade issues on which they should take a stand. Peoples' characters are run down in their presence, and they put in no dissenting word. Lewd pictures are put up in the places they work; obscene shows come to their town; vulgar, violent and sensuous literature is sold in places where they do much business, and they utter not a word of remonstrance or protest or indignation. Any issue that is unpleasant is avoided. Let the Herods of this world decide on those issues. They may well decide in the wrong way, but at least the vexing problems are shoved aside. To some extent, practically all of us engage in the practice of sending Christ to Herod.

When, not too much later in the morning, Jesus came back to stand for a second session before Pilate, Herod declining the responsibility of judgment, Pilate quickly went on to compromises that were more positive. There were two main compromises, both doing grave injustice to Our Lord.

Inglorious Comparison

First there was the giving of a choice between Jesus and Barabbas. It was customary to release a prisoner on the feast day. Pilate now thought of this and chose a man who was a robber, a murderer and a seditionist. Here evidently was somebody the people would think twice about before having him set free among them.

It probably took some time for the enemies of Our Lord to rally enough support among the crowd to shout for the release of Barabbas. It seems that it was during this interval of waiting that Pilate's wife, Claudia Procul (the name according to apocryphal gospels), sent a message to him telling him to have nothing to do with this just Man, for she had suffered many things in a dream because of Him that very day. This warning did nothing to help Pilate, but served only to

make him more uneasy and more ready to do
something to release Our Lord.

As a result of Pilate's offer, Jesus was put on an
equal basis with a known robber and murderer.
Pilate lowered a man he believed innocent to comparison with a criminal, hoping this would give
him an excuse to release Jesus. The motive was
good, but the act was unjust and evil in itself. It
was a compromise, and it backfired. Convinced in
some way by the active enemies of Our Lord, the
crowd shouted approval of the release of Barabbas in preference to Jesus.

A Drastic Step to Final Injustice

Then Pilate went on to a more injurious compromise. He had Our Lord scourged. It seems that
he had suggested this previously and then had
backed away from such a drastic step when the
custom of freeing a prisoner occurred to him. But
when that failed, Pilate returned to the expedient
of scourging Christ. Though scourging was the
normal preliminary to crucifixion, in the case of
Our Lord the scourging was intended originally
by Pilate to be merely something to satisfy Jesus'
enemies. He hoped thereby to stop short of actual
crucifixion. This was now going far in the wrong
direction, about as far as one could go without
going all the way to an unjust sentence of death.

Scourging was a cruel attack on the body; it
was painful, sometimes permanently injurious to
health, sometimes actually resulting in death. It

left a man branded in disgrace. The welts of the whips might heal in time, but the scars would remain on one's flesh the rest of his life, as well as the infamy of it—deserved or undeserved. All this Pilate was willing to do, paradoxically, in order to save Our Lord.

Modern Scourgers

The modern parallel to this is striking. This is the very procedure of those who approve and promote contraception. In order to obtain an apparently good end, they advise a means which is evil in itself. In order to produce "more healthy offspring," to provide them with the necessities and comforts of life, to take care of their educational needs, to enable them to live decently, to save them from the squalor and moral dangers of poverty, the propagandists speak out for sin. Pilate's way of trying to save Our Lord was certainly odd, to say the least. The way to the preservation of human and even spiritual values taken by the advocates of the sin of contraception, for example, is likewise certainly odd, to say the least. Pilate delivered Our Lord to be scourged in order to save Him. Today He is again delivered to be scourged by the sin of impurity in order to preserve the values He would have favored. In fact, some who have the name of followers of Christ have declared that sometimes there is a duty to practice the sin of contraception. Here is the exact parallel to Pilate. Christ must be scourged so that the spiritual life of Christ in man may be preserved!

But Pilate had more insight than the modern scourgers. He knew he was wrong. They at least profess that they do not know. Pilate took a basin of water and washed his hands, saying: "I am innocent of the blood of this just man; look you to it." (*Matt.* 27:24).

Hate Wins over Pity

The crowning with thorns was not done by order of Pilate. It was a joke of the rough soldiery. But it made even more of a sorry spectacle of Jesus. Hoping this sad sight would satisfy the enemies of Our Lord and stir up pity in the more neutral element of the crowd, Pilate brought Jesus forth and presented Him, saying: *Ecce homo!*—"Behold the Man!" (*John* 19:5). But the tide of emotion and of hate in the crowd had risen too high for it to be appeased by even the sight of Jesus flogged and crowned with thorns. It swept all before it. The crowd cried out: "Crucify him! Crucify him!"

Pilate answered this outcry by telling the multitude: Why don't *you* crucify Him. I myself can find no guilt in Him. In the new and savage heat of partial victory, the Jewish leaders then brought forth the original charge of perverting their nation, and explained just what they meant. "We have a law; and according to the law he ought to die, because he made himself the Son of God." (*John* 19:7).

Pilate Worried

At the very beginning of Our Lord's trial, this charge had been ignored by the governor. Now he is upset, especially when he hears the mention of "Son of God." He goes back inside and in his usual, direct way asks Jesus: "Whence art thou?" (*John* 19:9). No answer was given, since Our Lord had sufficiently explained to Pilate that He had a spiritual kingdom and had come into the world to bear witness to the truth. Pilate, however, was greatly fearful and reminded Jesus that he had the power to release Him or to crucify Him. Here the usual positions of judge and accused were turned around. It was the judge who was fearful and agitated. The Accused was calm and actually more in charge of the situation than anybody. To Pilate's worried question, Our Lord gave a forthright and yet a kind answer. He reminded Pilate that any power he exercised was only by permission of a power higher than any earthly power. "Thou shouldst not have any power against me, unless it were given thee from above." (*John* 19:11). Then He told Pilate that those who had delivered Him had committed the greater sin.

The Gospel writers are precise and brief. They do not give all the details, but soon sweep on to the conclusion of the trial, telling us that Jesus was delivered to be crucified. St. John has one short indication, however, that at this point, Pilate must have made a mighty effort to save Our Lord. St. John says: "And from henceforth Pilate sought to release him." (*John* 19:12). John says this as casually as if before this point, Pilate had not done so. Evidently, then, Pilate, fearful of some unknown divine power, full of respect for the calm, dignified Prisoner, completely convinced of His innocence and of the hatred and injustice of the accusers, made a stronger final effort to save the life of Christ.

Pilate Puts Self First

The enemies of Our Lord reacted by making the case a personal matter for Pilate. "If thou release this man, thou art not Caesar's friend. For whosoever maketh himself a king, speaketh against Caesar." (*John* 19:12). Pilate had already been reported to "Caesar," the Emperor Tiberius, and had been ordered to remove the gilt shields that offended Jewish religious sensitivity. Positions were lost and heads fell easily in those days. Pilate could not risk the damage that this aroused and determined group might do him. He saw that they were masters of deceit, unscrupulous and full of hate. When the full force of their hate turned from Our Lord to him, he, Pilate, might well lose all he most valued in life. So the issue resolved itself into choosing between himself and Our Lord. Pilate chose himself.

Here again is a clear picture of the final issue in all sin. The sinner chooses himself in preference to God. He chooses to keep his position bought by the sacrifice of principle, his unlawful married partner, his unjust gain, his rankling jealousy or hatred, his secret impure pleasure, rather than obey the law of God. It sounds cruel to put things this way, but in the last analysis, all sin is utter selfishness. The sinner chooses himself and delivers Jesus, Our Saviour, to be crucified.

Once the issue is clearly defined as a choice between condemning Jesus or incurring the grave risk of losing his job, Pilate quickly makes up his mind. He sat down in the judgment seat. This was in the paved court of the Antonia, an area of more than fifty yards square. The Greek word for this area was *Lithostrotos,* which means "paved place." The Hebrew word for this place, *Gabbatha,* means "high place," which is well suited because this was the highest point on the eastern side of the city. Excavations have uncovered this area.

Pilate knew he was beaten. Still, he dallied momentarily. He ironically pointed out Our Lord: "Behold your king." (*John* 19:14). This was no real effort now to save Jesus. Pilate expected the reaction that followed: "Away with him; away with him; crucify him!" Yet Pilate still asked in irony: "Shall I crucify your king?" The chief priests then gave the answer that was so humiliating to them: "We have no king but Caesar." (*John* 19:15).

Ibis ad Crucem

Pilate sat in his folding chair, his curule. It was about 11:00 a.m. The official way to give the sentence was to have it written and then read it. The penalty of crucifixion was usually designated by the words *Ibis ad crucem*—"You shall go to the cross." Whether Pilate used these exact words we do not know. It is likely that whatever he had written contained a reference to Our Lord as "Jesus of Nazareth, King of the Jews," for this is what he wrote to be placed over Jesus' head on the Cross. Pilate was occupied with the thought of Christ as King of the Jews, and he had this title placed on the Cross in three languages. Whatever the official written sentence of execution said, it likely contained the exact phrase: Jesus of Nazareth, King of the Jews. Having signed the official, written order, Pilate turned Our Lord over to the execution squad of four Roman soldiers with a centurion in charge.

Four Requests

Pilate was not yet done with this business. He had washed his hands to claim his own innocence in condemning Our Lord. He would have gladly now washed his hands of anything connected with Jesus' execution and burial. Yet he was approached three more times on Friday and once on Saturday about matters concerning Him.

First, the Jewish leaders came and protested about the title placed over the Cross. They wanted the wording changed from "JESUS OF NAZARETH, KING OF THE JEWS" to a form that would read: "He said, 'I am the King of the Jews.'" But Pilate was no longer to be pushed around. He gave a terse answer, worthy of a better man: *Quod scripsi, scripsi!*—"What I have written, I have written." (*John* 19:19-22). He had gone the whole way by giving in and condemning Jesus. Having done so, now, as with all weak men, he is suddenly firm on a minor point.

No doubt he enjoyed their discomfort and chagrin at having this title kept on the Cross, if we can speak of Pilate's enjoying anything that Friday. At least we owe it to Pilate that today we can look at our crucifixes and read the letters, I N R I, and know that in the hour of bitter defeat, in the hour of the triumph of falsehood, there remained the victory of a true proclamation on the Cross: "Jesus of Nazareth, King of the Jews."*

Pilate was bothered a second time by the Jewish leaders. They came about 3:00 p.m., "the ninth hour," to ask that the legs of the crucified might be broken. This would greatly hasten death. It was customary, and Pilate granted the request in view of the approaching feast day.

The third caller on Pilate was Joseph of Arimathea, a member of the Sanhedrin, a wealthy man, and a disciple of Jesus. He did something that took courage, considering the circumstances of that day. He went in and asked for the body of Jesus. Pilate wondered that Jesus should already be dead, since he had just granted the request of the Jews for the breaking of the legs of the three crucified men. So he sent for the centurion and

---

* *Jesus Nazarenus, Rex Judaeorum.* In Latin the letter "I" is often used for "J." —*Publisher, 2002.*

learned from him the fact of Christ's death. Then he granted Joseph's request.

The following day, Pilate was asked by some of the priests and Pharisees to set a guard about the tomb. He simply told them to use the soldiers already at their disposal. They had their own Temple guards, and at this time they must have still had the use of the cohort mentioned on Thursday night, or at least part of it.

The Gospels say no more of Pilate's further thoughts or activities. What his reaction was on hearing that Jesus had risen from the dead, what he may have done later to follow the beginnings of the new religion founded by Our Lord is not known.

No Friend of Caesar

Pilate sacrificed principle to save position. But his place of earthly power did not last long. After a few short years, he put down a rebellion in Samaria, but he did so with more force than necessary. Complaint was brought against him by the Samaritans and he was reported by Vitellius, the Roman legate of Syria, to Tiberius the Emperor. Pilate was summoned to Rome to stand before Caesar, the very thing he had sacrificed principle and the life of Jesus Christ in order to avoid. Tiberius died before Pilate reached Rome, and the succeeding Emperor, Caligula, confirmed the act of Vitellius in removing Pilate from office, then sent him into exile in Gaul. This was in A.D. 37.

There are two opinions on Pilate's final years. One has it that he became a Christian and led a holy life. The other says that he brooded with anguish until he committed suicide. The only definite thing that can be said is that we do not know. Pilate's burial place is pointed out as being on a mountain near Lucerne, Switzerland. This too cannot be proved.

Where Compromise Leads

Pilate wanted power and position. Perhaps he dreamed of lasting fame. His memory has come down to us, but his fame is an ill fame. He has been called cruel and overbearing as a governor, yet he did last ten years in a proud and rebellious land. Three uprisings in that time would not stamp him as cruel; neither would his final removal. Judging from his conduct on Good Friday, he was not cruel and vicious in the sense that he enjoyed or reveled in cruelty. He was not coarse, but rather penetrating in logic, and though a pagan, he showed more conscience than the Jewish leaders, who had divine revelation to guide them. Still, he was cruel in the sense that he permitted and even commanded gross injustice when it was expedient and useful.

Pilate is the classic picture of a man who will sacrifice principle to expediency, who will compromise on moral issues. Such people may be naturally inclined to justice, goodness and kindness, but they end by being just as cruel as the most vicious and violently disposed, due to their weakness and pusillanimity or cowardice.

Thus, Pilate stands in history as the man who went from compromise to compromise, to final cruelty. He tried to evade the issue of justice by sending Jesus to Herod. He proposed a choice between Barabbas and Our Lord. He had Our Lord scourged. He proclaimed Jesus' innocence and then made a show of proclaiming his own. He did everything but what was simply morally right. That is why he ended by joining forces with the enemies of Jesus, preferring temporary security to justice, to moral integrity and to an innocent Man's life.

Once a person begins to compromise he may end by doing what he had least hoped to do. He may drive himself into a corner of his own making, until he commits the greatest of sins and crimes. Pilate compromised. That is why today we repeat the sad truth as we say these words in the Apostle's Creed: "suffered under Pontius Pilate." May God have mercy upon his soul—and also upon our own, if we ever compromise with the truth.

Prices subject to change.

Forty Dreams of St. John Bosco. *Bosco* 15.00
Blessed Miguel Pro. *Ball* 7.50
Soul Sanctified. *Anonymous* 12.00
Wife, Mother and Mystic. *Bessieres* 10.00
The Agony of Jesus. *Padre Pio* 3.00
Catholic Home Schooling. *Mary Kay Clark* 21.00
The Cath. Religion—Illus. & Expl. *Msgr. Burbach* 12.50
Wonders of the Holy Name. *Fr. O'Sullivan* 2.50
How Christ Said the First Mass. *Fr. Meagher* 21.00
Too Busy for God? Think Again! *D'Angelo* 7.00
St. Bernadette Soubirous. *Trochu* 21.00
Pope Pius VII. *Anderson* 16.50
Life Everlasting. *Garrigou-Lagrange* 16.50
Confession Quizzes. *Radio Replies Press* 2.50
St. Philip Neri. *Fr. V. J. Matthews* 7.50
St. Louise de Marillac. *Sr. Vincent Regnault* 7.50
The Old World and America. *Rev. Philip Furlong* 21.00
Prophecy for Today. *Edward Connor* 7.50
Bethlehem. *Fr. Faber* 20.00
The Book of Infinite Love. *Mother de la Touche* 7.50
The Church Teaches. *Church Documents* 18.00
Conversation with Christ. *Peter T. Rohrbach* 12.50
Purgatory and Heaven. *J. P. Arendzen* 6.00
Liberalism Is a Sin. *Sarda y Salvany* 9.00
Spiritual Legacy/Sr. Mary of Trinity. *van den Broek* 13.00
The Creator and the Creature. *Fr. Frederick Faber* 17.50
Radio Replies. 3 Vols. *Frs. Rumble and Carty* 48.00
Convert's Catechism of Catholic Doctrine. *Geiermann* 5.00
Incarnation, Birth, Infancy of Jesus Christ. *Liguori* 13.50
Light and Peace. *Fr. R. P. Quadrupani* 8.00
Dogmatic Canons & Decrees of Trent, Vat. I 11.00
The Evolution Hoax Exposed. *A. N. Field* 9.00
The Priest, the Man of God. *St. Joseph Cafasso* 16.00
Christ Denied. *Fr. Paul Wickens* 3.50
New Regulations on Indulgences. *Fr. Winfrid Herbst* 3.00
A Tour of the Summa. *Msgr. Paul Glenn* 22.50
Spiritual Conferences. *Fr. Frederick Faber* 18.00
Bible Quizzes. *Radio Replies Press* 2.50
Marriage Quizzes. *Radio Replies Press* 2.50
True Church Quizzes. *Radio Replies Press* 2.50
Mary, Mother of the Church. *Church Documents* 5.00
The Sacred Heart and the Priesthood. *de la Touche* 10.00
Blessed Sacrament. *Fr. Faber* 20.00
Revelations of St. Bridget. *St. Bridget of Sweden* 4.50

Prices subject to change.

Prices subject to change.

At your Bookdealer or direct from the Publisher.
Call Toll Free 1-800-437-5876   ***Fax 815-226-7770***

Prices subject to change.

Fr. Christopher Rengers, O.F.M. Cap.

BORN in Pittsburgh in 1917, Fr. Christopher received his elementary education at parochial schools in Pittsburgh and then attended Capuchin seminaries for high school and theology. He entered the Capuchin novitiate in Cumberland, Maryland in 1936, made his first vows in 1937 and final vows in 1940. He was ordained in Washington, D.C. on May 28, 1942. He obtained an M.A. in history from St. Louis University, taught four years, then served as a chaplain and did parish work for over 50 years on various assignments in Kansas, Missouri, Ohio, Maryland and Washington, D.C.

Fr. Christopher's writings include books entitled *The 33 Doctors of the Church*, *The Youngest Prophet* (on Jacinta Marto), *Mary of the Americas*, *The Seven Last Words* and *Saints and Sinners of Calvary*, as well as magazine articles in *Our Sunday Visitor*, *Soul*, *Priest*, *Pastoral Life*, *Homiletic and Pastoral Review*, and *Extension*.

Since 1970 Fr. Christopher has been active in the St. Joseph Medal Apostolate and its related group for the laity, The Workers of St. Joseph, both of which he founded. This work includes fostering devotion through a medal of St. Joseph and its literature, making available materials on Our Lady of Guadalupe and arranging retreat-pilgrimages to her shrine in Mexico City.

The combined effect of this devotion to Joseph and Mary is directed to a flowering of new devotion to Jesus present in the Blessed Sacrament. The "Joseph way of life" is well expressed in the Workers' "Sum-up Prayer":

(*Continued* . . .)

May Joseph with hammer-blow my soul re-make
In pleasing pattern of Mary's choice.
So all I do is done for Jesus' sake,
And echoes clear the Father's voice.

Fr. Christopher is stationed at St. Francis Friary (Capuchin College) in Washington, D.C. His current apostolates include ministering to nursing home residents and helping with hearing Confessions at the nearby National Shrine of the Immaculate Conception.